SUPERSTARS
AND
MONOPOLY WARS

NINETEENTH-CENTURY
MAJOR-LEAGUE
BASEBALL

THOMAS GILBERT

THE AMERICAN GAME
FRANKLIN WATTS
A Division of Grolier Publishing
New York / London / Hong Kong / Sydney
Danbury, Connecticut

Photographs copyright ©: Transcendental Graphics: pp. 6 (Museum of Art, Rhode Island School of Design), 46, 79, 87, 106, 126, 141; National Baseball Library and Archive, Cooperstown, N.Y.: pp. 35, 38, 51, 55, 72, 101; Milwaukee Art Museum, Purchase, Layton Collection: p. 48.

Library of Congress Cataloging-in-Publication Data

Gilbert, Thomas W.
Superstars and monopoly wars : nineteenth-century major-league baseball /
Thomas Gilbert.
p. cm. — (The American game)
Includes bibliographical references (p.   ) and index.
Summary: Discusses the growth of baseball in the nineteenth century from
its enjoyment as a casual game to its commercialization.
ISBN 0-531-11247-0
1. Baseball—United States—History—19th century—Juvenile literature.
[1. Baseball—History—19th century.] I. Title. II. Series: Gilbert, Thomas W.
American game.
GV863.A1g576 1995
796.257'0973—dc20   95-31413 CIP
                                                                    AC

CONTENTS

CHAPTER ONE

Force Play: The Short Life and Times of Baseball's First Major League

Two centuries after the Pilgrims landed at Plymouth Rock, Americans finally got around to inventing a national sport—baseball. The basic idea of baseball had always been there; going all the way back to the Middle Ages, English-speaking children had been playing bat-and-ball games that resembled baseball. It was not until the 1840s, however, that baseball was taken up in a serious way by adults. The first formal match between two adult baseball teams took place on June 19, 1846, at a park named the Elysian Fields in Hoboken, New Jersey. One of the teams was a group of New Yorkers who called themselves the Knickerbockers; they were led by Alexander Cartwright, who, like most of the players, was a Wall Street clerk in his twenties. The Knickerbockers played baseball twice a week, on Tuesday and Thursday afternoons, as a way to loosen their limbs after long days spent sitting behind a desk. They wrote the first real baseball rules and organized the first baseball club.

Once baseball got started, it grew by leaps and bounds. By the middle 1850s there were a dozen base-

A Thomas Eakins watercolor, Baseball Players
Practicing, *dated 1875*

ball clubs in New York City and Brooklyn, which were then independent cities. When the Civil War broke out, baseball New York–style was being played in Philadelphia, Baltimore, Boston, and throughout the Northeast. At this time, baseball was still strictly amateur; no one made a living by playing baseball, and no one had to buy a ticket to watch a game. In the 1860s, however, this began to change, as more and more clubs found that they had to pay their star players or risk losing them to a club that would. Harry Wright's 1869 Cincinnati Red Stockings, the first club to pay regular salaries to all of its players, created a national sensation by undertaking a series of coast-to-coast national tours and going undefeated for nearly a season and a half. Cincinnati's June 1870 extra-inning loss to the Brooklyn Atlantics ended the unbeaten streak at more than seventy games. Partly because of the success of the Red Stockings, baseball became increasingly divided over the issue of pay for play. In 1871 baseball's governing body, the National Association of Base Ball Players (NABBP), split into two factions: the amateur majority, consisting of several hundred clubs that opposed paying their players, and the professional minority, made up of a small number of the top clubs that wanted to hire the best players available and sign them to contracts the way the Red Stockings had. On Saint Patrick's Day of that year representatives of ten clubs met in Collier's Bar in New York City to form a new organization called the National Association of Professional Base Ball Players, or National Association (NA) for short. The first professional league, the NA was the direct ancestor of our modern major and minor leagues.

Barely twenty-five years after Alexander Cartwright and a dozen of his fellow New York bank clerks had taken a casual children's game and adapted it for the recreation of grown-ups, teams of polished professional athletes from cities across the country were battling for major-league championships and batting titles before crowds of cheering fans. There were umpires, managers, and pennant races; fans pored over box scores and statistics in newspaper sports sections. Baseball was already considered the national pastime.

The amateur NABBP, baseball's first national governing body, was so loosely organized that it could not be called a league. There was no official schedule or clear way of determining a championship. And almost anybody could join; virtually the only requirements were that member clubs be all white and able to pay membership dues. In the end, this lack of organization proved fatal. The NABBP was done in by three main problems: a pervasive atmosphere of hypocrisy caused by the NABBP's sticking stubbornly to its amateur pretensions while more and more players and clubs turned professional; gambling-related corruption of players and whole clubs; and the growing phenomenon of players revolving, or jumping from one team to another— sometimes in mid-season—in search of better pay.

When Harry Wright and others formed the National Association in 1871, they were determined to set up a stronger, more disciplined organization that would be able to withstand these problems. They certainly had the right idea, but as it turned out, they did not go far enough. The result of their efforts was a sort of baseball Frankenstein monster—an ultimately unworkable structure that stood halfway on professional baseball's evolutionary scale between the chaotic NABBP and today's tightly organized major-league monopoly.

The NA had a fairly high standard of play—high enough that most historians today accept the NA as a major league—and a loose sort of schedule. Teams could schedule games as they wished, but they were supposed to complete a certain number of series with each other by the end of the season. And the NA certainly solved the problem of hypocrisy on the issue of professionalism: it proudly proclaimed its status as a professional organization. However, although the NA central office was given powers undreamed of by the officers of its predecessor, it was not very successful in dealing with corruption or disputes over player movement. When the NA self-destructed after five seasons, largely as a result of these two problems, it became clear to Harry Wright and his fellow baseball entrepreneurs that baseball needed to run a much tighter ship, under an even stronger central authority.

Today baseball and gambling are separated by a wide gulf that few players dare to cross. When they do, as in the case of Pete Rose, baseball comes down on them like a ton of bricks. On the basis of some fairly flimsy evidence that he might have bet on baseball games, Rose was banned from baseball for life in 1989. As unfair as the Pete Rose banishment might seem, there is certainly plenty of precedent for it in baseball's recent history. Commissioner Bowie Kuhn banned retired baseball legends Willie Mays and Mickey Mantle from working in major-league baseball for years because they did some minor promotional work for an Atlantic City casino. Brooklyn Dodgers manager Leo Durocher was suspended for the entire 1947 season merely for socializing with gamblers and organized crime figures. In 1943 Commissioner Kenesaw Mountain Landis threw Phillies owner William Cox out of baseball for placing a small bet on his own team to win. Most players today are conditioned to avoid the slightest contact with gamblers, and most fans would be utterly shocked to find out that any of their heroes were involved with gambling in any way. The reasons for baseball's almost paranoid fear of being contaminated by gambling go back to the Black Sox scandal of 1920, when members of the Chicago White Sox admitted that they had taken money from gamblers to throw the 1919 World Series, and even farther back to a rash of similar scandals in the 1910s.

The 1870s, however, were a different world—a world with a much higher tolerance for gambling. Gambling pervaded American society throughout the middle nineteenth century to an extent that modern Americans would have difficulty comprehending. Few nineteenth-century sports fans would have thought it possible to separate sports from gambling, even if it had occurred to them that it might be a good idea to do so. In the 1850s, for example, the NABBP had to deal with fan complaints about umpires betting on games. The association's response was not to prohibit gambling by umpires but to pass a rule that all bets were off on a game in which the umpire was found to have a financial stake in the outcome. Gambling was also much more socially acceptable in nineteenth-century America than it is today. Middle-class and upper-class women fans bet openly on baseball games during the Fashion Course series of 1858. In the 1870s Brooklyn's Union Grounds, the finest ballpark of the day and the site of many NA games, added a special facility *inside the ballpark* for the use of bookmakers and set aside a section of the grandstand for the comfort of gambling fans.

The founders of the National Association believed that open professionalism would solve the gambling problem. If players were paid salaries, they thought, then players would have little incentive to risk lucrative professional careers by fixing games for gamblers. Unfortunately, crookedness had become thoroughly ingrained in too many players; the NA was beset by one gambling scandal after another. New York Mutuals pitcher Bobby Matthews and three teammates were accused of throwing games in 1874; that same year an NA umpire, Billy McLean, revealed that he had heard several players plotting to fix games. The names of stars

George Zettlein, John Radcliff, and Bill Craver came up again and again in accusations of game fixing. Even though NA rules stated clearly that any player found guilty of corruption was to be banned from baseball for life, the NA central office did its best to sweep most such charges under the rug. Matthews, Zettlein, Radcliff, and Craver went unpunished. The message went out to other NA players that corruption would be tolerated. Throughout the NA's five seasons of existence, public confidence in the integrity of professional baseball plummeted. Journalists openly scoffed at suspicious plays and umpiring calls and hinted broadly in their baseball stories that games were being rigged.

Gambling was not the only problem that the NA central office failed to solve. Alcoholism was also rampant among NA players; drinking may have affected the outcome of more games than dishonesty. Numerous players, including pitching stars Cherokee Fisher and Bobby Matthews, were known to have missed games because of hangovers or to have played while drunk.

As corrupt as many of its players were, however, the worst influence on the NA turned out to be the behavior of some of its own member clubs. Because of financial problems or sheer indifference to association rules, few clubs bothered to complete the minimum number of series with each club required for an official season. This also eroded the prestige and authority of the NA central office. In 1874, for example, NA clubs were supposed to play ten games against each opponent, for a total of 70 games. While the first-place Boston club played exactly 70 games, only one other club completed more than 60; the last-place Lord Baltimores went 9-38, finishing 31½ games out of first place.

This was actually a relatively good showing by an also-ran NA club. Because of the association's lax admission standards, dozens of weak clubs with no hope of competing for the championship came and went during the NA's five seasons; sometimes their only purpose was to schedule a few home games against a strong opponent that would draw fans, make a quick buck off ticket sales, and then disband before their first road trip. Some of the worst NA seasons include the Washington Nationals' 0-11 performance in 1872; the Brooklyn Eckfords' 3-26 record in that same year; and the Brooklyn Atlantics' 2-42 mark in 1875.

It was not only the weak clubs that undermined the integrity of the NA schedule. In July of 1874 the NA's two top clubs, Boston and Philadelphia, decided to sail across the Atlantic Ocean to play a series of exhibition games, both baseball and cricket, in Great Britain and Ireland. Planned by Harry Wright and Albert Spalding as a way to demonstrate American athletic superiority to the world's greatest sporting country, the trip was a mixed success. Ticket sales were disappointing, and English fans showed little enthusiasm for the game of baseball. Thanks to the presence of experienced cricketers like English-born Harry Wright, his two brothers, George and Sam, and Jim "Orator" O'Rourke, the Americans did manage to win a few of the cricket matches. Whatever the tour may have done for baseball abroad or for America's sporting reputation in England, it devastated the NA season. The Red Stockings and Athletics did not return home until the middle of September. Not only did the trip leave a gaping two-month hole in the NA schedule, but it also killed fan interest by entirely upstaging the NA pennant race in the sports pages. Attendance at NA games in August fell below the 1,000 mark, and the New York Mutuals, who were strong contenders for the pennant, were regularly outdrawn at home by amateur and sandlot contests.

The biggest fiasco in the history of the NA—the Davy Force affair—was another case in which the association was corrupted from within by its stronger franchises. The founders of the NA had intended to solve the problem of players revolving, or jumping from one team to another, by requiring clubs to respect each other's contracts and forbidding them to sign any player who had been expelled by another club for disciplinary reasons. Revolving did not disappear, however; it simply took another form. Instead of a situation in which players went from team to team for their own reasons as in the NABBP days, in the NA period clubs brazenly raided each other's rosters. Western clubs like William Hulbert's Chicago White Stockings complained that it was impossible for them to compete because the wealthier eastern powerhouses regularly stole their players. In the Davy Force case and dozens of similar cases, powerful NA clubs like the Red Stockings and Athletics lured away players already under contract to opponents or signed ineligible players. When the victims of these maneuvers protested to the NA central office, the Bostons and Philadelphias threw their political weight around and pressured the NA to rule in their favor.

At five feet four inches, 130 pounds, Davy Force was a small man, even by the standards of a century ago. An inch and a half shorter and ten pounds lighter than fellow nineteenth-century great "Wee Willie" Keeler, he was nicknamed "Wee Davy" and "Tom Thumb," after circus promoter P. T. Barnum's famous dwarf. Force was, however, a terrific hitter for average. He batted .406 for Troy and Baltimore in 1872 and hit .326 over his five seasons in the NA. Later in his career Force bulked up to around 160 pounds; with the Athletics in 1875 he showed new power, hitting 21 doubles and 6 triples. Force was also a terrific fielder. In spite of an awkward bowlegged style that baseball writer Francis Richter compared to that of Honus Wagner, Force was considered by contemporaries second only to George Wright as a defensive shortstop. He also possessed a strong enough arm to play quite a few games at third base; he even occasionally pitched in relief.

In 1874 the twenty-five-year-old Force turned in a solid season for the White Stockings, playing third base and shortstop, and batting .314 with an impressive 61 runs scored in 59 games. Chicago finished a respectable fifth in an eight-team race, and in September of 1874 the team signed Force to a new contract for 1875. In early December, however, the Philadelphia Athletics offered Force a contract for 1875 at a higher salary. Force signed this contract as well. Both clubs claimed that they owned the rights to Force for 1875, and the matter was referred to the NA judiciary committee. On the first day of the NA annual convention, which was held before the start of the 1875 season, the judiciary committee decided to return Force to Chicago on the logical grounds that its contract had been signed first.

In his 1992 history of the NA, *Blackguards and Red Stockings*, historian William Ryczek tells the bizarre story of what happened next. Among the purposes of the NA national convention was the election of new officers for the upcoming year. This meant that there would be a new NA president and a new judiciary committee. Only a few hours after the outgoing judiciary committee made its decision in the Force case, Charles Spering of the Philadelphia Athletics was elected NA president. An indignant Spering refused to accept the decision returning Force to Chicago and convinced the assembled NA delegates to refer the matter to the incoming 1875 judiciary committee for reexamination. Named to the 1875 version of the committee were E. Hicks Hayhurst of the Philadelphia Centennials, Morgan Bulkeley of the Hartfords, Benjamin Van Delft of the Brooklyn Atlantics, George Concannon of the Philadelphia Pearls, and a man named Trimble representing the Keokuk, Iowa, Westerns. When Trimble had to bow out for personal reasons, NA president Spering seized the opportunity to appoint himself to fill the vacancy. The five-man judiciary committee, now stacked with an unshakable majority of three Philadelphians, reversed the 1874 committee's ruling and awarded Force to the Athletics. The committee based its decision on a routinely ignored NA rule that teams could not sign players to seasonal contracts until March 15, when their contracts for the previous season were up. Even though Philadelphia's contract with Force was also signed months before the March 15 deadline, the judiciary committee ruled, inexplicably, that Chicago had lost its right to Force by signing him too soon.

The bitterness that followed Spering's crude power play lasted well into the 1875 season. Boston manager Harry Wright proposed a boycott of games with Philadelphia and protested to influential sportswriter and national baseball authority Henry Chadwick. "How long," he wrote in a letter to Chadwick, "will the National Association exist if the clubs violate its laws with impunity when they conflict with their special interests?" Hartford protested its first game against Philadelphia, claiming that Force was ineligible. Even the fans registered their disapproval. Covering an early May game between the Atlantics and Athletics, the *New York Clipper* reported that while the Brooklyn crowd applauded good plays made by the other Athletics, Force's efforts were "received with silence."

Back in Chicago, watching his Force-less team finish 35 games behind Wright's Boston Red Stockings, White Stockings owner William Hulbert nursed the biggest grudge of all. The men who ran the NA did not know it, but in Hulbert they had made a very dangerous enemy. The Force case steeled Hulbert's resolve to plan a counterattack on the Philadelphia mafia that ran the NA as soon as the 1875 season was over. Before the opening of the 1876 season, Hulbert would succeed in destroying not only the power of the Philadelphians, but the entire National Association as well.

Off the field the NA left a lot to be desired. What was NA baseball like on the field? In a word: ragged. The NA may have been a lot more competitive than the

NABBP of the 1860s and 1850s, but the corruption and lack of discipline of the association's management structure were well matched by chaos between the white lines.

To understand baseball 1870s-style, it helps to think of modern Chicago sixteen-inch softball. With no home run fences to shoot for, batters tried to hit hot grounders or line drives through the infield for singles. Defenseless, bare-handed infielders tried to smother or knock down batted balls, then scramble to their feet and make a throw in time. To add insult to injury, official scorers were liberal about giving out errors; there were many times more unearned runs than in today's game, and good fielders compiled fielding averages that seem amazingly low by today's standards. Today good-fielding shortstops regularly retire with lifetime fielding averages above .970. The greatest shortstop of the NA days, George Wright, had a lifetime fielding average of only .917. Of course, modern shortstops have the advantage of using gloves. George Wright towered over his contemporaries as a fielder; he was the only short-stop to compile a lifetime fielding average over .900 until the 1890s—well into the glove era.

What made a player like Wright even more impor-tant to teams of the 1870s was the fact that the fair-foul hit forced infielders to cover much more ground than in today's game. Under NA rules, a batted ball was con-sidered fair if it bounced at least once in fair territory, even if it passed well on the foul side of first or third base. Hitters like perennial NA batting champ Ross Barnes learned how to direct "fair-foul" hits with regu-larity so far into foul territory that they would reach second or even third base before the ball could be retrieved. Thanks to this rule, Barnes hit .401, .422, .425, .344, and .361 in his five NA seasons.

Pitching was not nearly as important in the NA as it is today. Because few NA pitchers had mastered the art of the breaking pitch—pitchers did not begin to throw effective curveballs until the late 1870s—and because pitching velocity, at least with men on base, was severely limited by the ability of the gloveless and pad-less NA catchers to stop the ball, batters held a distinct advantage. With few batters striking out and most spraying one hot shot after another at the infielders, the most important thing in determining who won and who lost an NA game was the ability of the infield to control the damage.

It is not surprising, then, that the team that dominated the NA, winning four out of five of its pennants, was the team with the finest defensive infield: Harry Wright's Boston Red Stockings. The Boston infield was anchored by the NA's best fielder and best all-around player, George Wright. In fact the only season in which the Red Stockings failed to win the NA pennant, 1871, was also a season that George Wright sat out with a leg injury. At first base was Charlie "Bushel Basket" Gould, who was famed for his ability to dig throws out of the dirt; at second was sure-handed Ross Barnes; catching was cannon-armed Cal McVey; and at third was Harry Shafer. Just as winning seems to follow good pitching around in today's baseball, in the 1870s winning seemed to follow the slickest infielders. Three members of Boston's state-of-the-art infield, for example—McVey, Wright, and Gould—had formed the nucleus of the undefeated Cincinnati Red Stockings of 1869 and 1870, and two of them—Barnes and McVey—went on to play for the 1876 Chicago White Stockings, the first National League champions.

If the fair-foul hit sounds a little silly to the modern fan, it is nothing compared to the rest of the NA rules. In 1873, for instance, the NA introduced a rule aimed at stopping fielders from catching balls in their hats; evidently fielders had been doing this in order to spare their perpetually bruised hands and fingers. The rule stated that if a fielder made a catch using his hat, the batter would be awarded first base and the ball would be considered dead until returned to the pitcher on the mound. The problem with this rule became obvious in a game between the Red Stockings and Athletics in Philadelphia. In the bottom of the ninth, with the bases loaded and none out, the Philadelphia batter hit an easy pop fly to shortstop George Wright. Wright caught the ball in his cap and flipped it to pitcher Al Spalding on the mound, putting it in play; Spalding threw to catcher McVey, who threw it to third baseman Shafer, who sent it on to second baseman Barnes for what the Red Stockings claimed was a 6-1-2-5-4 triple play. Only the threat of a riot by the Philadelphia fans prevented the umpire from agreeing.

Other comical items from the NA rule book include the 1872 rule that "a batter shall be privileged to use his own private bat exclusively. No player of the opposing club shall have any claim to the use of the bat except by consent of the owner"; the 1871 rule allowing substitute runners, even to run for batters from home to first, by the consent of the opposing captain; the 1874 rule settling the burning issue of which team was to provide the game ball—the visiting club for a series of games, the home team when a single game was played; and the 1874 rule stating that "should the umpire be unable to see whether a catch has been fairly made, he shall be privileged to appeal to the bystanders and render his decision according to the fairest testimony at command." All in all, the picture that emerges from the NA rule book is of something closer akin to a pickup softball game in the park than to a modern major-league game.

One particular game that seems to sum up the disorganized state of baseball NA-style is the Philadelphia-Baltimore contest played in Baltimore on May 20, 1872. The game was scheduled to begin at two o'clock, but a dispute over the selection of the umpire caused a delay. By NA rules, the umpire was to be an unpaid volunteer acceptable to both sides. Because there was only one umpire in an NA game, choosing the right man was very important. Scandals involving incompetent or dishonest umpires plagued the association throughout its existence. In 1873, for example, NA president Robert Ferguson, who was umpiring a game between Baltimore and the New York Mutuals, got into an argument with the Mutuals catcher, picked up a bat, and broke the catcher's arm in two places. A policeman who was sitting in the stands ran out and tried to arrest Ferguson, but the catcher, perhaps understandably, refused to press charges against his league president.

The problem on May 20 was that neither side could agree on an umpire. Both teams vetoed a number of suggested candidates and a standoff ensued. Finally, after a two-hour wait, the Athletics agreed to accept a young player named Graham from the Baltimore Olympics, a non-NA club, and the game began. By the second inning, however, the inexperienced Graham was already beginning to lose control of the game. The Athletics were a rough bunch that included tough guys like Bill Craver, who was later banned from baseball for life for fixing games, and Adrian Anson, then known as "Baby" for his incessant complaining and umpire-baiting. Sensing that the umpire was becoming intimidated, the Baltimore crowd rose in anticipatory protest after every close play. In the eighth inning, a Baltimore player pulled the hidden-ball trick on an Athletic base runner who thought, mistakenly, that umpire Graham had called time out. When Graham ruled the runner out, the Athletics refused to come out for the bottom of the inning. The game ended with angry fans mobbing the playing field. Even though the score stood 7–4 in favor of Baltimore and it was the Athletics who had forfeited the game by walking off the field, the NA later ordered the game replayed from the beginning.

CHAPTER
TWO

$\mathscr{B}$orn in Rebellion: The Owners' League

A middle-aged businessman who by 1876 had built a successful wholesale grocery and coal supply business, William A. Hulbert made an unlikely revolutionary. With his large but distinctly pudgy frame, he made an even more unlikely baseball man. Born in 1832 in Burlington Flats, New York, a small village not far from the current site of the National Baseball Hall of Fame and Museum in Cooperstown, Hulbert moved to Chicago with his family when he was two years old. By his late thirties, he was a respected member of the Chicago Board of Trade.

Hulbert was an energetic civic booster—"I would rather be a lamppost in Chicago than a millionaire in another city" was his favorite expression—when that booming young city was nearly destroyed by the Great Fire of October 1871. One of the worst disasters in U.S. history, the Great Fire killed more than 250 people and obliterated three and a half square miles of downtown Chicago. It destroyed almost 18,000 buildings and left more than 150,000 people without homes or jobs. The city might never have recovered, but Hulbert and men like him were determined to rebuild Chicago into the major American city—an economic and cultural rival to New York, Philadelphia, Boston, and the other eastern metropolises—that it had been on the way to becoming when the fire struck.

Baseball was part of their plan. As in the 1860s when the success of the Cincinnati Red Stockings inspired imitators across the country, being competitive on the national baseball scene carried with it a great deal of prestige. In the 1870s, a city that aspired to major-league status in American culture or in the American economy, also aspired to compete on the major-league baseball diamonds of the National Association and, later, its successor, the National League.

As a result, Chicago's comeback as a city can be traced not only in the business sections of contemporary newspapers but also in the sports pages. The Chicago White Stockings were tied with Philadelphia in the race for the 1871 pennant when the Great Fire destroyed the team's ballpark, clubhouse, equipment, and even their uniforms. Many players lost their homes and everything they owned. The same was true for most of the team's financial backers. Instead of forfeiting the rest of the season, however, the Chicago White Stockings accepted the NA's offer of free rail passes and spare uniforms and equipment collected from the rest of the league. The Chicago players gamely completed the rest of their schedule in one long road trip; in spite of this hardship, they finished only two games behind the pennant-winning Athletics.

Two years passed before Chicago was financially able to field another NA team. William Hulbert was only one of many stockholders in the 1874 White Stockings, but within a year he moved up to director and then team president. By 1875 the city of Chicago was nearly all the way back, and Hulbert was about to make sure that the eastern baseball powers that had dominated the NA knew it. As historian Lee Allen wrote:

> *Chicago in the 1870s was a boisterous bawd, filled with brash optimism and majestic plans. Following the disastrous fire that ate out the city's heart, a new metropolis was arising and spreading to the prairie. The sound of hammers was heard everywhere. The atmosphere was electric with a crackle of promise that signaled the boom. It was a time and place for fearless men who knew exactly where they were going. Bill Hulbert, although then a minor figure in the city's life, was one of these.*[1]

As far back as the first few months of the 1875 season, Hulbert plotted what Albert Spalding later referred to as their "rebellion." Hulbert had two purposes: one was to reform baseball by replacing the weak, ineffectual NA with a strong owner-dominated system based on sound business principles; the other was to make the Chicago White Stockings the best baseball team in America. On the reform front, Hulbert planted a series of articles in the *Chicago Tribune* in the fall of 1875 that criticized the status quo in baseball and called for change. Most of the top clubs, including the Chicago White Stockings, according to the *Tribune*, were losing money by being forced to play second-rate NA clubs that did not draw fans. If "the whole gang be let in" in 1876, the result would be financial disaster. The *Tribune* suggested that it might be a good idea for the top clubs to withdraw from the NA and form their own closed corporation.

Meanwhile, Hulbert was going about the business of improving the White Stockings in a much less public way. He secretly approached Albert Spalding, the star pitcher of Harry Wright's Boston Red Stockings dynasty, and urged him to come home. Hulbert appealed to

Spalding's regional loyalty, a feeling that had not entirely disappeared among baseball players of the 1870s even after five or more years of professionalism in baseball. "You've no business playing in Boston; you're a western boy and you belong right here," Hulbert told Spalding. This struck a responsive chord in Spalding, who later described his first meeting with Hulbert as follows:

> [Hulbert] seemed strong, forceful, self-reliant. I admired his businesslike way of doing things. I was sure that he was a man of tremendous energy—and courage. He told me of the interest of Chicago in baseball; how that thousands of lovers of the game at Chicago were wild for a winning team, but couldn't get one; how she had been repeatedly robbed of her players, and, under Eastern control of the Professional Association, had no recourse. It seemed to me that he was more deeply chagrined at the insult to Chicago than over that city's failure to make a creditable representation in the game.[2]

For Spalding, who came from Rockford, Illinois, the idea of playing in his home state was not the only attraction of Hulbert's proposal. Hulbert had also offered Spalding a glimpse of a very promising future away from the playing field. Spalding was to serve as manager and captain as well as starting pitcher for the 1876 Chicago team, but he was also to serve in an executive role, as Hulbert's right-hand man if and when his new boss launched a new major league. This appealed to Spalding because, even though he was only twenty-five and the first pitcher in history to record 200 major-league victories, the truth was that he was becoming bored with playing baseball. One reason for his boredom was the Red Stockings' amazing success.

"Our nine," Spalding wrote in his 1911 autobiography, "had won the pennant three years in succession and had it cinched for the fourth. It was becoming monotonous." Another reason was the fact that Spalding could see that in Hulbert's version of baseball's future, the real money would be made by the baseball men wearing business suits, not those wearing flannel knickers.

The idea of helping to set up a new, more stable major league and exploiting the vast commercial possibilities of the growing sport of baseball seemed much more exciting to Spalding than pitching another 70-game season. Sure enough, after going 48-13 the following year to pitch the White Stockings to the first National League pennant, the twenty-six-year-old Spalding retired to move into the Chicago front office and to found a sporting goods business on the side. It was baseball's most shocking retirement until Sandy Koufax quit pitching at age thirty after going 27-9 with a 1.73 ERA for the 1966 Los Angeles Dodgers. It was also a very shrewd move; before he was out of his thirties, Spalding was president and part owner of the Chicago White Stockings, the de facto leader of the National League, publisher of baseball's official annual, official supplier of NL baseballs, owner of the worldwide Spalding sporting goods empire—and a millionaire.

After Spalding signed his secret contract to play for Chicago in 1876, Hulbert sent him back to Boston to try to recruit as much as possible of the nucleus of the Red Stockings. Under the nose of unsuspecting Boston manager Harry Wright, Spalding persuaded Ross Barnes, Deacon White, and Cal McVey—Boston's three biggest stars, after Spalding himself and George Wright—to sign secret contracts to play with Chicago in 1876. Spalding, Barnes, White, and McVey later became known as the Big Four. Spalding and Hulbert did not stop there; from the Philadelphia Athletics, the team that had stolen Davy Force, they plucked hard-hitting Adrian Anson, an emerging star. The players were offered large raises to go to Chicago, but regional pride might also have played some part in their decision; except for White, who was from the Buffalo area in upstate New York, all of them were from Iowa or Illinois.

The NA, of course, had a rule that players could not be signed until March 15 of that same season. Because of this, Hulbert and Spalding intended to keep their player signings strictly secret. Unable to restrain itself from crowing about Chicago's great coup, however, the *Chicago Tribune* spilled the beans after only two weeks. Boston fans were outraged. "Seceders!" they yelled at the members of the Big Four; this was a stinging insult in those days only a decade after the end of the Civil War. There were no lasting hard feelings on the part of Boston management, who, according to Deacon White, made no attempt to keep the players by matching Chicago's "fancy western prices," but Bostonians remained bitter. Not even the Red Stockings' finest season ever—in 1875 the "seceders" led the team to a 71-8 record, 18½ games ahead of second-place Hartford—mollified the Boston fans. More ominously, the Philadelphia Athletics were unhappy and there was talk around the league that the NA central office might intervene and possibly even expel the Big Four and Anson for the 1876 season.

This was just what Hulbert was waiting for: an excuse to take on the whole NA structure. "I have a new scheme," Hulbert told Albert Spalding. "Let us anticipate the eastern cusses and organize a new association before the March meeting, and then we'll see who will do the expelling." Hulbert and Spalding got to work designing a formal constitution for a new league that would be called, not the National Association of Professional Base Ball Players but the National League of Professional Base Ball Clubs, or the National League (NL). The new title was symbolic of a very real difference.

The new league would be a strong centrally controlled organization of clubs, not of players. There would be strict admission criteria to keep out the second-rate clubs that had weakened the NA; only clubs that came from cities with 75,000 or more inhabitants and could pay annual dues of $100 were eligible to join. The NL was also to be very much a closed corporation; any two member clubs could blackball, or bar entry to, any new club wishing to join the new league. As in any other business, there would be a clear separation between labor and management—with management firmly in charge. Never again would a player serve as a league president, as Robert Ferguson had done in the NA. In Hulbert and Spalding's league, players would play and capitalists like Hulbert would make all off-field and business decisions.

Hulbert had carefully prepared for his next move, which was to confront the old NA directly. He and Spalding softened up potential opponents like Harry Wright and Henry Chadwick by casting themselves as reformers, determined to cleanse baseball of the gambling, drinking, and other forms of corruption that men like Wright and Chadwick had been wringing their hands about for years. Hulbert met secretly with representatives of key western franchises in Cincinnati, Louisville, and St. Louis. With those teams on board, he then traveled to New York City and arranged a meeting with the eastern clubs.

The meeting took place on February 2, 1876, at the Grand Central Hotel, which was located only a few blocks from the bar where the NA had been founded in 1871. When Hulbert got up to speak, the men from Boston, Philadelphia, and New York knew what he was going to say—and how little they could do about it. Because he had already put together a solid majority of supporters, Hulbert was able to offer his plan for a new league as a virtual fait accompli. The National League,

Hulbert declared, had three objects: "first—to encourage, foster and elevate the game of baseball; second—to enact and enforce proper rules for the exhibition and conduct of the game; and third—to make Base Ball playing respectable and honorable." The NA was formally dissolved, and the meeting ended with all of the clubs—Chicago, St. Louis, Hartford, Boston, Louisville, New York, Philadelphia, and Cincinnati—agreeing to Hulbert's proposals in their entirety and following his suggestion to appoint Hartford club president Morgan Bulkeley, an eastern ally of Hulbert's, as the first NL president. William Hulbert's revolution had created a new order in baseball: the National Association was dead and the new capital of the baseball world was Chicago.

Even though Morgan Bulkeley served as president for the first year of the NL's existence, there was never any question that he was a figurehead. William Hulbert was the real boss of baseball after 1875. Starting in 1877 Hulbert took over from Bulkeley and served from then on both as league president and as president of the Chicago White Stockings. Hulbert ruled with an iron hand, expelling players and whole clubs that did not live up to his personal standards and establishing the principle that major-league baseball should be run as a business monopoly by and for ownership. Hulbert died unexpectedly of a heart attack in 1882 at the age of fifty, but he had lived long enough to see his creation, the National League, grow and prosper. Oddly, Hulbert appears to have seriously delayed his deserved election in the Baseball Hall of Fame by his appointment of Bulkeley as the NL's first chief executive. Before the Hall of Fame opened in 1939, a committee was charged with selecting a group of "pioneering executives," who were to join the first group of players to go in. The committee, which had clearly not done much serious research, ignored Hulbert in favor of the insignificant Bulkeley, who left baseball in 1877 to pursue a career in Connecticut state politics. This mistake was finally remedied when William Hulbert was elected to the Hall of Fame by the Veterans Committee in 1995.

In many ways, modern major-league baseball is a product of events that occurred between 1876 and 1881. In 1876 William Hulbert founded the first modern league. In 1877 the first minor leagues were formed. In 1879 Hulbert introduced the reserve clause, which tightened the owners' grip on baseball and ended most contract-jumping by binding players to their teams indefinitely and which became the focus of bitter labor-management conflicts in baseball for a century. In 1881 a rival major league, the American Association, was founded, and baseball was on the verge of its first war over the major-league monopoly.

The more some things in baseball changed, however, the more others remained the same. An example of the latter was gambling-related corruption. In spite of William Hulbert's strong words about discipline and honesty, and in spite of new mechanisms like the black-list, under which no player expelled for drinking, throwing games or other disciplinary reasons by one NL club could be signed by another NL club, the NL soon found that it contained crooked players, just as the NA and the NABBP had.

Dishonest players may well have been encouraged when Hulbert admitted the unsavory New York Mutuals into the NL in 1876. The Mutuals featured second baseman Bill Craver and pitcher Bobby Matthews, two players with dubious reputations going back to their NA days. After the 1876 season ended, Hulbert asserted the central authority of the league in the strongest possible terms when he expelled NL franchises from the nation's two largest cities, New York and Philadelphia, for failing to complete season-ending road trips—something that had been widely tolerated in the NA days. In 1877 the Louisville club gave Hulbert an opportunity to show whether he meant what he said about not tolerating gambling and crooked play.

In the late summer of 1877 Louisville was 3½ games up on Harry Wright's Boston Red Stockings and seemingly well on the way to clinching the NL pennant. The team was led by ace pitcher Jim Devlin, who finished the season with 35 wins and a 2.25 ERA, and featured two members of the 1876 Mutuals: second baseman Bill Craver and utility man Al Nichols. Then came a very suspicious-looking losing streak; before they knew it, the surprised Red Stockings were seven games in the lead.

During the losing streak, Louisville club officials noticed that there had been unusually heavy telegraph traffic to and from several of their players, including Nichols. They confronted Nichols, insisted that he open all of his wires, and discovered that gamblers from New York City were paying Devlin, Craver, Nichols, and star outfielder George Hall to throw the pennant race. Devlin, Nichols, and Hall confessed, and Hulbert banished all four men from the NL for life. For years afterward, Craver, who always maintained his innocence, and Devlin, who had been a good friend of Hulbert's, came to the NL annual meetings and begged, in vain, for reinstatement. Both eventually gave up and began second careers in law enforcement—Craver in Troy, New York, and Devlin with the Philadelphia police department.

Hulbert's decisive handling of the Louisville scandal helped the reputation of the league in the long run, but it created a great deal of short-term chaos. Both Louisville and St. Louis, which had signed the four guilty players to contracts for the 1878 season, joined Hartford in dropping out of the NL. These three teams were replaced by Providence, Milwaukee, and Indianapolis. Hulbert was finding it difficult to avoid the kind of franchise instability that had plagued the NA; in just three NL seasons, his league had gone from eight teams to six and had contained eleven different clubs.

The NL began to turn this around beginning with its return to an eight-team format in 1879. The clubs were Providence, Boston, Buffalo, Chicago, Cincinnati, Cleveland, Syracuse, and Troy. With the exception of Cincinnati, which was expelled in 1881 and replaced by Detroit, and Syracuse, which gave way to Worcester, Massachusetts, in 1880, there were no further franchise disruptions until the restructuring brought about by the compromise that ended the war between the NL and the American Association in 1883.

During this period Hulbert's firm leadership of the NL began to bear fruit. The new league had sold the nation's fans on its new, cleaner brand of baseball. Part of this success was due to the effective handling of the Louisville situation, but the NL had demonstrated a commitment to higher standards in other areas as well. Off the field, open gambling and the sale of alcohol were strictly prohibited at all NL parks, and fan rowdiness was swiftly and surely dealt with. On the field, for the first time in baseball history, umpires were paid and a stable, professional umpiring crew was created.

Americans responded to the new order in baseball. Attendance went up, as fans of a new generation of baseball stars passed in ever greater numbers through major-league turnstiles. (The turnstile, incidentally, was invented in 1878.) Because of rule changes, or perhaps simply because of age, many of the stars of the NA days faded. Spalding, of course, retired in 1877. George Wright could not learn how to hit the curve ball; although he continued to excel in the field, he never hit .300 in the NL. When the fair-foul hit was done away with by a rule change in 1877, Ross Barnes's career went into a permanent nosedive; after hitting .429 with 21 doubles and 14 triples in 1876, Barnes dropped to .272 with one extra-base hit in 1877. Cal McVey retired after the 1879 season. Dickey Pearce, the inventor of the bunt and one of the first great shortstops, finally quit playing in 1877 at the age of forty-one. Replacing these names were great players like catcher Deacon White, who got his nickname from the fact that he did not drink, smoke, or gamble; Adrian Anson, who would become baseball's first 3,000-hit man; Jim "Orator" O'Rourke, a strong-armed right fielder who hit .331 for the 1870s and had the decade's highest seasonal RBI total with 62; and Irish-born pitcher Tommy Bond, who took Spalding's place in Boston in 1876 and reeled off three 40-win seasons in a row. With a strong, stable major-league monopoly made up of competitive franchises spread across the country from Boston to Chicago to Cincinnati, William Hulbert's vision had been realized: the national pastime had never been more "respectable and honorable"—or more profitable.

CHAPTER THREE

"What a Glorious Sight It Was!": Cap Anson and the Chicago Dynasty

William Hulbert was the visionary who built the first modern major league—and built it to last. Of the five major leagues that were launched in the nineteenth-century, only his National League is still around today. Hulbert created a disciplined, owner-dominated system that has maintained its grip on the major-league baseball monopoly for 119 years.

Major-league baseball, however, is more than a set of business arrangements between franchises. It is what major-league players do on the field of play that captures the imagination of the public, sells tickets, and builds generations of loyal fans. Great feats and individual records, thrilling pennant races and World Series showdowns, mighty dynasties and fierce rivalries—these are the ingredients that, through layers of memory, accumulate to create the enduring mystique of major-league baseball. "Mystique" is the right word, because part of what the major leagues have always sold to fans is the idea that its players are not just professional athletes but larger-than-life heroes possessing special qualities of determination, courage, and character.

The major-league mystique is a phenomenon that builds on itself through the continuity of the major leagues and their franchises. Records are important because they enable today's players to be measured against those who have gone before; team dynasties set the standard for the great teams that come after them. As they root for their favorite teams and worship their favorite players, youngsters are drawn into the world of baseball; inspired by their idols, they grow up to take their children to see ball games. Some of them complete the cycle by becoming major-league players themselves.

The future of Hulbert's National League was not ensured until it produced a bona fide national hero, a player whose exploits captured the hearts and minds of American sports fans and who became the idol of every boy and girl with a bat and ball. That player was a brash, handsome midwesterner named Adrian Constantine "Cap" Anson. Anson's father, Henry Anson, had settled temporarily in Michigan on his way from Dutchess County, New York, to the West, and apparently he missed Michigan (Cap Anson's first and middle names, as well as those of his brother Sturgis Ransome Anson, were also the names of small southern Michigan towns). Cap Anson had a close-cropped military mustache, blue eyes, light hair, and an extremely fair complexion— he was also known by the nickname "Swede"—and he was physically huge; at six feet two, 220 pounds, he remained the largest man in baseball for most of his career. He had a rough edge that may have come from the primitive conditions of his upbringing among the Pottawattomi Indians in Marshalltown, Iowa, on what was then the western frontier, but Anson was clearly a fighter and a leader by nature.

One of the players who had been lured to Chicago in 1876 by Albert Spalding, Anson took over as player-manager of the White Stockings in 1879. Anson was a relentless competitor, an innovative manager, and a tremendous judge of baseball talent. In a 1928 book called *The Great Teams of Baseball*, veteran sportswriter MacLean Kennedy describes Cap Anson as follows:

> *Anson was one of the greatest drawing cards of his time. He always received a hearty reception. Perhaps not always as a friend or popular hero, yet he received unusual attention when he headed his great team around the circuit. The more hostile the reception the harder he fought to win. Bold, fearless, he fought for his rights in the open. More than anything else, the fans liked Anson to kick [abuse the umpire]. Be it said right here that the big leader never lost a chance to deliver an oration, which always ended with an admonition to the opposition, the umpire and sometimes to the occupants of the stands.*[1]

Anson became a national celebrity to a degree that no baseball player before him could have imagined. Youngsters traded Cap Anson tobacco cards, copied his trademark open stance, and gripped their Cap Anson bats with their hands spread apart, in imitation of their hero. "To hit like the big Chicago giant," remembered nineteenth-century sportswriter Sam Crane, "or at least to imagine so, was glory enough for all time." Anson batted .300 or higher twenty times in his twenty-two-year NL career; he had hit well over .300 in each of his five NA seasons as well. He remained in the public eye for so long that, over time, he came to be known by three different nicknames: Baby, for his nonstop complaining and umpire-baiting, and in ironic reference to the fact that, as sportswriters loved to repeat, Anson was the first white baby born in his Iowa hometown; Cap, for captain after he became Chicago's player-manager; and finally Pop, when he continued to play well into his forties. His retirement in 1898 was so unthinkable to

A. C. "Cap" Anson (center in striped coat)
with the Chicago White Stockings of the early 1880s

White Stockings fans that the team became known for a few seasons as the Orphans. In 1900 Anson started a not-so-glorious tradition by publishing baseball's first as-told-to jock autobiography. It was a best-seller.

Anson's White Stockings of 1880–1886 were baseball's first dynasty. This was a team that had it all: great hitters like Anson himself, speed burners like George Gore and Abner Dalrymple—it was because of players like these that the team was also nicknamed the "Colts"—slick fielders like Ned Williamson and Silver Flint, and superb pitchers like Larry Corcoran, Fred Goldsmith, and John Clarkson. Anson and the White Stockings were giants in more ways than one; with at least six regulars who were five feet eleven or taller in a time when the average major leaguer was closer to five-eight or five-nine, the team literally towered over the rest of the National League. The White Stockings even had an all-star team of sorts of drinkers and playboys like King Kelly, Gore, and Jim McCormick—and outfielder Billy "The Parson" Sunday, who quit baseball and became a popular evangelist.

Under Anson's leadership, his team won five pennants in seven years. There was nothing in baseball like Anson's White Stockings until the advent of the New York Yankees dynasty in the 1920s and 1930s. It was not only Anson's official achievements in the NL that made his face as recognizable to most Americans as Abraham Lincoln's. Throughout the 1880s and 1890, Anson and his team crisscrossed the country, playing local and small-town teams in exhibition games before, during, and after the regular season. In those days before movies, radio, or television, these so-called barnstorming trips added much to the Anson legend, and they were invaluable in promoting and establishing the young National League. For several baseball generations, Anson and his team *were* the major leagues. William Hulbert may have built the business of major-league baseball, but Anson more than anyone else built the romance and the mystique that have made the major leagues a cherished national institution for more than a century.

After the glorious season of 1876, when Albert Spalding pitched and managed Anson and the Big Four to the NL's first pennant, the team quickly fell apart. Deacon White returned to Boston; Ross Barnes's career was ruined by the rule change that outlawed the fair-foul hit; and Spalding quit pitching. After coming in second to last in 1877, Spalding quit managing, too, to run the White Stockings' front office and to concentrate on his sporting goods business. Under Spalding's successor, NA veteran Bob Ferguson, the team made little improvement, finishing in fourth place with a record of 30-30. William Hulbert then put Anson in charge of the White Stockings for the 1879 season.

Anson conducted a thorough housecleaning, bringing in four players from Indianapolis, including catcher Silver Flint, third baseman Ned Williamson, outfielder Abner Dalrymple from Milwaukee, and a young outfielder from Maine named George Gore, whom Anson had spotted in an exhibition game in Massachusetts. This team also finished fourth, but with a much-improved won-lost mark of 46-33. Anson moved himself from third base to first and batted .396 to win the NL batting title by a margin of 39 points over Providence's Paul Hines.

The great Chicago White Stockings dynasty began with Anson's first pennant as a player-manager in 1880. Further strengthened by the additions of all-around offensive force Mike "King" Kelly and pitchers Larry Corcoran and Fred Goldsmith, Anson's team won 21 of its first 22 home games and never looked back, coasting to a record of 67-17, fifteen games out in front of second-place Providence. Chicago's 1880 winning percentage of .798 remains an NL record to this day.

Thanks in part to Hulbert's reserve clause, which kept players under contract as long as their teams wanted them, Anson was able to keep together the core of the 1880 team well into the second half of the decade. A look through the lineups of Anson's teams shows that the Chicago White Stockings of 1880–1886 were a finely tuned and powerful baseball machine, perfectly suited for baseball 1880s-style, which emphasized speed, baserunning, infield defense, control pitch-

Anson's 1885 Chicago White Stockings

ing, and hitting for average. Taking their lead from Anson himself, the White Stockings were a smart, tough, and durable outfit, and they put together an amazing run of success, winning the NL pennant in 1880, 1881, 1882, 1885, and 1886 and finishing second in 1883. They were also as colorful a collection of characters as baseball has ever seen.

Batting cleanup and playing first base was the mighty Anson himself. Anson does not fit the modern image of a cleanup hitter, mainly because he hit only 96 career home runs; he hit none or one in a season ten times. Compared to a modern slugger like Reggie Jackson or Cecil Fielder, Anson had virtually no home run power at all. Of course, in the 1880s neither did anyone else's cleanup hitter. Like a lot of his contemporaries, the right-handed Anson held his hands slightly apart on the bat and poked at the ball instead of taking a big uppercut swing from the heels. There were two reasons for this: fast outfielders and big outfields. At that time outfield fences, if there were any, were located so far from home plate as to be unreachable, even for a man as strong as Anson; outfielders could easily run under most fly balls that today would carry into the seats. A majestic modern-style home run shot, climbing into the sky like a rocket and falling to earth 425 feet away, was no fan souvenir in Anson's day—it was just another out. A good RBI man was expected to spray line drives all over the field with as much consistency as possible; line drives through the infield produced singles, and line drives into the outfield gaps produced doubles and triples.

This is exactly what Anson did better than almost anyone. "When Anson hits the ball it *travels*," reads an 1886 game story in the *Chicago Journal*, "It does not linger at any point along its line of route but cuts the air on its way to the goal the big fellow intended it to reach, with a warning screech that most infielders have the highest possible respect for."[2] He hit for average, batting .334 lifetime and winning three batting titles. He regularly hit over 25 doubles and between 5 and 15 triples in a season. In the bottom-line statistic of runs batted in, Anson led the league four times and totaled over 100 six times—this while playing seasons of between 112 and 139 games. He led all hitters in total RBIs for the decade of the 1880s, with 803.

Playing second base for most of Cap Anson's teams was tall, mustachioed Fred Pfeffer, a skilled and reliable defensive player who anchored the White Stockings' "Stonewall Infield." While Pfeffer at one time held many fielding records—he is still number one all-time in total chances per game at second base—he also had decent power and was considered a good clutch hitter. Anson liked to bat him fifth, where he usually drove in around

80 runs despite batting in the middle .250s. Like most of the rest of Anson's lineup, Pfeffer also had outstanding speed; in 1885 he won a race around the bases against five of the fastest men in baseball with a time of 15¾ seconds.

Anson's catcher was Frank Flint, known as "Silver" for his white-blond hair. Flint did not hit much; in fact, he routinely batted after the Chicago pitcher. Hitting, however, was not very high on the list of qualifications for a major-league catcher's job in the 1880s. Guts were. Playing without masks or padding of any kind, Flint and his fellow receivers were expected to stop balls in the dirt, aggressively try to snare foul tips, and, with men on base, play directly behind the plate, as the well-armored modern catcher does. Even though more and more players began to use fielding gloves during the middle 1880s, these gloves bore no resemblance to the padded basketlike modern mitt. Made of very thin leather and sold in pairs, with the fingertips on the throwing hand cut out, they were more like handball gloves, offering some protection against bruises and calluses but no help at all in catching the ball. For a catcher, this kind of glove made little difference. Under these conditions, it is hard to believe that Flint was able to catch the vast majority of White Stockings games for nine years, from 1879 to 1887; during the four-year period between 1879 and 1882, Flint worked an utterly amazing 314 of the 337 games that Chicago played. It is less amazing that, over the course of his career, Flint was reported to have broken every major bone in his face and both hands.

Alternating at third base and shortstop were Tommy Burns and big Ned Williamson. Burns was an above-average fielder and a smart, aggressive player who relished blocking runners off bases. Williamson was a husky, extremely muscular player with a good glove and a strong arm. Quicker on his feet than he looked,

Williamson ran the bases well and hit for decent average, with occasional outbursts of power. He was ahead of his time in that he was extremely patient, content to draw a base on balls if the pitcher refused to give him a good pitch to hit. When you run down his seasonal hitting statistics, two numbers jump out: Williamson's 49 doubles in 98 games in 1883, and 27 home runs in 107 games the following year. Both figures led the league by wide margins. In fact, no major leaguer had ever hit anywhere near 27 home runs in a season before, and none would again until Babe Ruth hit 29 thirty-five years later, in 1919. As amazing as these numbers are, however, they are more a reflection of Ned Williamson's intelligence and versatility than of his true power.

The explanation for Williamson's power explosion of 1883 and 1884 lies in the strange layout of Chicago's Lakefront Park, the White Stockings' home, which was rebuilt for the 1883 season. The brainchild of William Hulbert and Albert Spalding, Lakefront Park was the first ballpark intended to draw fans by catering to their comfort and convenience. Previous ballparks had been slapdash, purely utilitarian structures thrown together out of boards and two-by-fours. Lakefront featured grandstand seats "elevated . . . so as to command the best view of play" (cushions were available for a small charge), sumptuous luxury boxes for the wealthy—Spalding's private box even contained the latest thing in office technology, a telephone—and a carved wooden pagoda that served as an entranceway. Every exposed surface was freshly painted and new. The ballpark held 10,000 fans, more than any other baseball facility in the country, and the White Stockings had little trouble filling it; throughout the early 1880s Anson's team drew the most fans in the NL, often averaging several thousand per game for a season.

The new park also featured a six-foot-high right-field fence that was only 252 feet from home plate in right center and 196 feet down the line. For the sake of comparison, Fenway Park's legendary "Green Monster," the closest outfield fence in the major leagues today, is 379 feet from home plate in left-center and 315 feet down the line; it is also 60 feet high, including the screen on top. Because Lakefront Park's 1883 ground rules made balls hit into the right-field seats a double, the right-handed Ned Williamson altered his swing so that he could take virtually any pitch in the air to right. He managed to hit more ground-rule doubles than any of his teammates, including the lefties. In 1884 the White Stockings changed the rule to make a fly ball over the fence in right field a home run. Once again Williamson took better advantage than anyone. After the team moved out of Lakefront the following year, Williamson's power numbers dropped off sharply, although in 1887 he did manage to rebound to hit 20 doubles, 14 triples, and 9 home runs in a more conventional ballpark.

The final member of the Stonewall Infield was King Kelly, who served as a super-sub type of utility man, along the lines of Tony Phillips with the Detroit Tigers of the early 1990s. Kelly played shortstop, caught when Silver Flint needed a rest, and played the outfield as well. His real importance to the White Stockings, however, was as a multifaceted offensive weapon. A tall, wavy-haired second-generation Irishman with dark eyes and a flowing mustache, Kelly was an exciting player who brought fans out to the ballpark not only with his style of play but also with his showmanship. Kelly loved to play to the crowd, whether it was exchanging insults with hecklers or serenading the Irish section of the St. Louis bleachers, known as the Kerry Patch, with his rendition of "The Battle of the Boyne Water," the anthem of Ulster Protestants. An incredibly popular star among the largely Irish Boston fans in 1888, Kelly may well have served as the model for the swaggering hero of Harvard-graduate Ernest Lawrence Thayer's famous poem "Casey at the Bat," which first appeared in print that year.

A terrific line-drive hitter and a dashing base runner, King Kelly was the Rickey Henderson of his day. He led the NL in doubles three times and in batting averages twice; he hit .307 for his sixteen-year major-league career. He was also a run-scoring machine, leading the NL three times in runs for Anson's White Stockings and, in one incredible stretch, scoring 399 runs for Chicago in only 333 games between 1884 and 1886. Although stolen base records were not kept for the first nine years of his career, Kelly stole 315 bases in the seven seasons he played after his twenty-eighth birthday. Like Henderson, Kelly was not the fastest base runner of his time, but he was the smartest and most daring.

Kelly had a creative streak that sometimes crossed the line into cheating. His most famous innovation was the hook slide, or the Chicago slide, as it became known after the rest of Anson's speedsters picked it up. Kelly's invention baffled a generation of middle infielders and inspired a popular song called "Slide, Kelly, Slide." Among Kelly's less legitimate inventions were his tactic of dashing directly across the diamond from first to third when he saw that the umpire—at this time, there was still only one working most NL games—had his back turned to watch a play in the outfield. He would also put bats or other equipment in front of the plate when an opposing runner was trying to score from third.

Some of Kelly's tricks were not illegal; they only seemed to be. For instance, during one game in which Kelly was not in the starting lineup, an opposing batter hit a foul ball out of reach of catcher Silver Flint but directly toward the Chicago bench, where Kelly was seated. Taking advantage of the contemporary rule that allowed player substitutions immediately upon an oral announcement, Kelly stood up, yelled "Kelly now catching for Chicago," and made the catch for a perfectly legal out. It was often said at the turn of the century that 90 percent of the baseball rule book had been written specifically to thwart trick plays dreamed up by King Kelly.

Unfortunately there was a dark side to King Kelly's playfulness and excess: he was completely irresponsible with money and a heavy drinker and gambler. While he was playing for Chicago—where Cap Anson enforced a strict training regimen, and kept Kelly under a particularly close watch by having his nighttime activities monitored by private detectives—Kelly kept his bad habits relatively under control. There were occasional lapses, though, like the time a stinking-drunk Kelly muffed an easy fly ball in the outfield to cost Chicago a game. Returning to the bench and seeing the angry looks on his teammates' faces, Kelly muttered, "By God, I made it hit me gloves, anyhow." By 1887, however, Anson was fed up and sold Kelly to the Boston Red Stockings for the unheard-of sum of $10,000. This only added to the Kelly legend; he was now known as the "$10,000 Beauty." Soon, however, Kelly's star began to fade. Overweight and firmly in the grip of alcoholism, Kelly left Boston after the 1892 season and drank himself to an early death in 1894. He was only thirty-six years old. "Time and time again," Cap Anson writes of Kelly in his autobiography, "I have heard him say that he would never be broke, and he died at just the right time to prevent such a contretemps from occurring."

Batting first and second for Anson's teams were a pair of left-handed speedsters, Abner Dalrymple and George Gore. Dalrymple was a poor left fielder, but in every other way he was a typical White Stocking—smart and aggressive on the bases and a consistent, durable hitter. As Anson's table-setter, he led the NL in at-bats and scored over 90 runs four times in the 1880s.

He batted .295 over his eight seasons with Chicago, with good doubles and triple power. The first of several major leaguers to be given the nickname "Piano Legs," center fielder George Gore was Dalrymple's superior in every area but one—personal character. Gore had blazing speed and a terrific batting eye; he led the NL in walks three times and in runs scored twice. He was one of the NL's top base stealers and a consistent .300-hitter, winning the 1880 batting title at .360 and hitting .300 or better seven times after that. Unfortunately, Gore seems to have spent more time training with King Kelly than with Cap Anson. Anson suspended Gore for drunkenness in 1885, replacing him with Billy Sunday, and released him to the New York Giants a year later. But in spite of his devotion to, as Anson put it, "women and wine," Gore did not self-destruct like his old friend Kelly. Gore went on to have several more fine seasons in New York before leaving the major leagues for good in 1892. He retired with 1,327 runs scored in 1,310 games; he is one of only three men in history to have scored more runs than games played over the course of an entire career. Even though Anson claims in his autobiography to have found him down and out on the streets of Manhattan during the 1890s, George Gore lived to a ripe old age. He died in Utica, New York, at the age of seventy-six.

One of the most famous members of Anson's White Stockings dynasty was outfielder Billy Sunday. What made him famous was not his baseball-playing, however, but his second career as an evangelist. The aptly named Sunday was an Iowa boy who had been recruited by Anson from the Marshalltown town team in 1883. He was probably the fastest man on the fastest team in baseball—he ran, Anson said, "like a scared deer"—and he was one of the NL's top base runners and base stealers. He was also an outstanding outfielder, regularly leading the league in statistical cate-

Outfielder Billy Sunday, who left the hard-drinking White Stockings to become a famous evangelist and a leading proponent of Prohibition

gories like put outs per game and total chances per game. However, Sunday never was able to break into the Chicago starting lineup. A weak hitter who struggled to keep his batting average over .250, he spent almost all of his five years with the White Stockings riding the bench or filling in as a fourth outfielder.

The spiritual turning point in Sunday's life came one day in 1887 when, walking the streets after a long night of partying with some of his fellow White Stockings, Sunday was startled by the sound of a mission choir singing hymns. Bursting into tears, he renounced his sinful ways, saying, "Good-bye, boys, I'm through. I'm going to Jesus Christ. We've come to a parting of the ways." He continued to play ball until 1890, but he quit drinking, smoking, and playing cards; he also refused to play baseball on Sunday.

After retiring from baseball at the age of twenty-seven, Billy Sunday went to work for the YMCA before setting out on his own as an evangelical preacher. Over the next two decades, traveling across the country and drawing crowds that would have made William Hulbert smile, Sunday became a national figure who was often credited with doing more than any other single person to make Prohibition a reality. He served as an example for future evangelists and televangelists to follow; Billy Graham and others still use many techniques devised or perfected by Billy Sunday.

One oddity of Sunday's oratorical style was his frequent use of baseball imagery. In his sermons, Christ throws fast balls at temptation and calls the devil out; sinners are left on base; and those who repent their sins slide—Billy Sunday would often physically run and slide headfirst across the stage to emphasize this point—into salvation. Billy Sunday never entirely severed his connection to baseball; he was a frequent spectator at major-league ballparks and loved to serve as a volunteer umpire in minor-league games.

A George Bellows painting, The Sawdust Trail, *depicts a 1917 Billy Sunday revival meeting.*

Anson's team included a lot of great players, but talent alone cannot account for five pennants in seven years. If a modern team put together a record like that of the White Stockings from 1880 to 1886, much of the credit would undoubtedly go to the organization that developed the homegrown players, the front office that signed or traded for key players from other organizations, and the manager who was able to keep the team motivated and focused on winning year in and year out. In the 1880s, however, there was no organization and no front office in the modern sense. In addition to playing first base, batting cleanup, and managing the games, Cap Anson also handled every other aspect of the game, with the exception of purely business matters. He performed the functions of a modern scout, public relations man and general manager. More than any modern manager, Cap Anson deserves the lion's share of the credit for his team's success.

Like all great managers, Cap Anson was utterly committed to winning. He kept his team in top shape through the toughest schedule of practices and workouts in the league. Anson pioneered the use of spring training, taking his team on annual preseason trips to Hot Springs, Arkansas. Austere in his own habits—Anson's wife Virginia had persuaded him to quit drinking back in his days with the Philadelphia Athletics—Anson was a disciplinarian who conducted nightly bed checks on the road and did not long tolerate players who refused to follow orders.

Anson was decisive when it came to personnel decisions, and because of his unerring eye for talent, there was always a good young prospect to take the place of a Kelly or a Gore. Unlike modern major-league teams, of course, the White Stockings could not simply reach down and grab a player from their farm system—there was no such thing in the 1880s. Chicago's "farm system" consisted of Cap Anson and the team's rigorous schedule of exhibition games against minor-league, college, and amateur teams across the country. Few future major-league players escaped Anson's discerning gaze, and many future White Stocking stars were scouted or signed by Anson at these games.

John McGraw, who had a successful major-league career and then, with the New York Giants, became one of the greatest managers of the twentieth-century, liked to tell the story of how in 1891 the great Anson spotted him during an exhibition game. At that time McGraw was a raw eighteen-year-old playing for a bush-league outfit called the Cedar Rapids Canaries. Completely in awe of Anson and the White Stockings, McGraw's teammates covered up their nervousness by razzing the White Stockings; McGraw in particular more than held his own in some rough give-and-take with the great Anson himself. Rounding first base, McGraw even dared to yell at Anson for blocking the base path. Fortunately, that day McGraw was able to back up his words; he robbed Anson of a hit with a nice catch and singled cleanly off Chicago pitcher Bill Hutchinson. At the end of the game, as McGraw told it, a suddenly friendly Anson approached him and asked if he would like to play for Chicago someday. McGraw never did play for Anson, but he did play against him as the star third baseman of the great Baltimore Orioles teams of the middle 1890s.

As a game manager, Anson was a nineteenth-century version of Billy Martin; with his great size, Anson was, if anything, more intimidating than Battling Billy. While his team was at bat, Anson would roam the baselines like a caged animal, clapping and shouting encouragement to his team and ridiculing and insulting everyone else in the park, from the umpire to the opposing team to hostile fans. Anson's temper was explosive and, at times, uncontrollable. During one game in the middle 1880s, Anson was nose to nose with an umpire who had made a

*Orioles third baseman John McGraw terrorized
opponents and NL umpires.*

controversial call against Chicago, when Al Spalding—
who had become the White Stockings' part owner and
team president after William Hulbert's death in 1882—
jumped out of the stands to join in. At this point an even
more enraged Anson turned on Spalding—his boss—
and told him between obscenities that this was *his* team

and *his* argument and to get back in his seat. Spalding did as he was told.

Bad temper or no, Cap Anson was a cool tactician and a creative problem-solver. His White Stockings excelled at the fundamentals of 1880s baseball; they were always on the cutting edge of innovations in base stealing and sliding techniques and in new offensive set plays like the hit and run. On defense, Anson took Harry Wright's idea of using outfielders to back up each other and to relay throws to the infield, and extended it. On Anson's team, both infielders and outfielders backed each other up on all throws. Because they had some of the first great curveball pitchers, the White Stockings were the first team to use signals for communication between pitcher and catcher.

Anson was also on the cutting edge when it came to handling pitchers. This was particularly important in the 1880s, a time of dizzying nonstop tinkering with the pitching rules. The pitching distance, the rules governing the strike zone, and the number of balls and strikes necessary for a strikeout or a walk—most of these were changing virtually on an annual basis. Some of the most profound changes were in pitching deliveries. The 1880s saw pitchers change from throwing dead underhand or submarine style, to sidearm, to three-quarters, and even to straight overhand. Each of these changes favored some pitchers and forced others to retire; managers were constantly forced to rebuild or reshuffle their pitching staffs. Anson's 1880 team had a two-man pitching staff of Larry Corcoran and Fred Goldsmith, both masters of the recently invented curveball. It was not a rotation; Corcoran pitched 63 games to Goldsmith's 26. As primitive as this arrangement sounds, it was in fact an innovation; recognizing that pitchers like Corcoran were straining their arms by pitching in the new sidearm style, Anson acquired a competent backup in Goldsmith and used him more than any other NL manager used his second pitcher. As recently as three years before, most teams had used only one starting pitcher. Even in 1880, Cleveland's Jim McCormick pitched all 74 of his team's games, using the old-fashioned submarine delivery that put little strain on the arm.

In 1881 and 1882 Anson stayed ahead of the trend by dividing the pitching work almost evenly between Corcoran and Goldsmith, employing what amounted to a two-man rotation. Corcoran responded by leading the NL in wins in 1881 and in ERA in 1882; in both seasons the two-man Chicago staff allowed the fewest runs in the league. Then, in 1884, Corcoran blew out his arm and Goldsmith began to fade; Anson quickly released them both and signed McCormick and John Clarkson, a right-handed control pitcher who had caught his eye at—where else?—an exhibition game against the Harvard College team. Clarkson helped the White Stockings to the 1885 pennant with one of the finest pitching seasons in history; he went 50-16 with a 1.85 ERA and pitched so well that Anson temporarily abandoned the idea of a two-man rotation. Number two pitcher Jim McCormick pitched only 24 of Chicago's 94 games in 1885, but did not hurt the team too badly, going 20-4. The following year Anson reversed field and became one of the first to experiment with a three-man rotation, conserving Clarkson's valuable arm by adding Jocko Flynn to the staff of Clarkson and McCormick.

The White Stockings dynasty ended after 1886. Although the team remained competitive for a few more years, Anson won no more pennants and Chicago spent most of the 1890s in the second division. But the memory of the glory years of 1880–1886 did not fade quickly. Chicago fans could still remember watching Anson, Kelly, Williamson, and the rest taking their positions in front of the huge adoring crowds at Lakefront Park and sensing from the look in the visiting team's eyes that, somehow, the game was already over.

As King Kelly remembered in an interview with the *New York Sun*:

> *There were seven of us six feet high, Anson, Goldsmith, Dalrymple, Gore, Williamson, Flint and myself . . . Only four of us had led the league in batting—Anson, Gore, Dalrymple and myself. We always wore the best uniforms that money could get, Spalding saw to that. We had big wide trousers, tight-fitting jerseys, with the arms cut clear to the shoulder, and every man had on a different cap. We wore silk stockings. When we marched on a field with our big six-footers out in front it used to be a case of "eat 'em up, Jake." We had most of 'em whipped before we threw a ball. They were scared to death.*[3]

For thousands—perhaps hundreds of thousands—of fans in the rest of the country, however, Cap Anson and his White Stockings were better remembered from a time when they played the local minor-league or town team on an off-day or during a barnstorming trip. In his 1950 memoir *My 66 Years in the Big Leagues*, former NL star catcher and longtime Philadelphia Athletics manager Connie Mack tells the story of the time the White Stockings came to his hometown, the grim New England mill town of East Brookfield, Massachusetts. Mack was a poor teenager working, as his Irish-immigrant father had before him, long hours in an oppressive shoe factory; even though he found the time to play on the town baseball team, Mack had no idea of ever escaping East Brookfield or playing professional baseball.

The manager of Mack's team had written to Anson, offering $100 if the White Stockings would play them on the way back from a regular-season series with Boston; to their shock, Anson accepted. Imagining how glamorous the White Stockings, a team coming off

Cap Anson's White Stockings on world tour of 1888–89. Anson is third from the left in the back row.

three straight NL championships, would look in their splendid red, white, and black uniforms, Mack and his young teammates spent the next several weeks working feverishly to clean up the garbage-strewn vacant lot where the game was to be played. The whole town was in a frenzy of anticipation when the White Stockings' train finally arrived. "It was a bigger event to us than the inauguration of a president," Mack remembers, "We cheered ourselves hoarse as Pop Anson and his Colts trotted onto our sandlot. What a glorious sight it was!"

C H A P T E R
F O U R

*B*eer, Whiskey, and the Reserve Clause: Monopoly Wars I and II

At the close of the 1881 season, the National League had, to all appearances, succeeded beyond anything William Hulbert or Albert Spalding could have hoped. Not only were more fans in more cities paying more money than ever before to watch major-league baseball, but the NL was an unchallenged monopoly. It had the major-league market all to itself, and with the adoption of the reserve clause, it had begun the process of gradually reducing the players to peons, with little control over their own careers and no say at all in industry-wide matters.

After the success of Hulbert's league, a number of other professional leagues had been formed; among the earliest were the International Association and the New England League, both founded in 1877. None of these, however, competed with the NL for top baseball talent; within a few years, most of them had fallen into an arrangement with the NL that resembled the relationship between today's major and minor leagues. For the most part, the leagues respected each other's player contracts and markets, and an understanding developed that the best players would eventually work their way up from the lesser leagues to the NL. During the late 1870s and early 1880s, more and more leagues and clubs joined the League Alliance, an organization sponsored by the NL that strengthened the NL's grip on the major-league monopoly by formalizing the major league–minor league relationship and creating the kind of league classification system that is seen in today's professional baseball, where minor leagues are ranked according to competitive level as Class AAA, Class AA, Class A, and Rookie.

Even better for Hulbert and Spalding, their team, the Chicago White Stockings, was the best draw in the NL, both at home and on the road. There was certainly no more profitable franchise in the country. According to historian Peter Levine, the White Stockings brought in gate receipts of between $23,000 and $32,000 in 1878, 1879, and 1880. How much money was that in the late 1870s and early 1880s? Consider that, according to the advertising pages of the 1880 *Spalding Official Base Ball Guide*, a baseball bat cost thirty-five cents, a pair of leather baseball shoes cost three dollars, a room in a first-class hotel cost between one and two dollars, and the guide itself sold for a dime. During and after the heyday of Cap Anson's dynasty, the team made even more money, reaping a reported $60,000 profit in 1888 and making many times that by speculating in real estate in Chicago and in the White Stockings' spring-time home of Hot Springs, Arkansas. The Chicago White Stockings, according to an 1888 story in the *San Francisco Examiner*, made "such profits yearly as would . . . make even bonanza kings envious."

In 1881, however, it was not only bonanza kings who were envious. A rapidly-expanding group of major-league-quality markets and wealthy investors were also eager to acquire major-league franchises, but they had been kept out of William Hulbert's closed corporation. In a pattern that would play itself out over and over again throughout the rest of baseball history, the owners who ran the major-league monopoly in the 1880s refused to expand to meet the economic demand. Instead of giving up some personal control over their industry by taking in new partners and exploiting new markets—which would have expanded the industry and made it more profitable—they preferred to remain big fish in a small pond. When the level of tension between those on the inside and those on the outside rose high enough, the result would be the formation of a new, independent major league. This would be followed by an all-out economic war over the valuable major-league baseball monopoly between the major-league establishment and the newcomer.

There was another way in which the heavy-handed monopolistic practices of the NL proved to be self-destructive by making Hulbert's league a tempting target for outsiders—the reserve clause. The reserve clause gave owners unprecedented control over player movement, but it also angered and alienated the players by taking away their freedom to choose where they wanted to play and by driving down their salaries. This had the unintentional effect of making it easier for new leagues to raid NL rosters and lure away underpaid NL players with offers of more money and more freedom; by hurting the players, the owners were actually hurting themselves, by lowering the value of their main asset.

The reserve clause was adopted as a way to prevent baseball owners from bidding against each other for players' services, thereby driving up the cost of doing business. Throughout the late 1870s, player salaries had indeed risen sharply for this reason. After the 1878 season, Providence hired George Wright and Orator O'Rourke away from Boston with hefty salary increases—and won the pennant. Many owners were alarmed at the prospect of other teams following Providence's example and driving up payrolls for everyone. In 1879 they decided to do something about it: they cheated. As historian Harold Seymour describes those days: "The owners soon realized what was causing high salaries. It was competition among themselves for players. Scrambling for men jacked up payrolls and boosted costs. The owners believed the existence of even the wealthy clubs was threatened, and indeed that of 'the whole professional fabric.'"[1]

If all this sounds familiar, it is because today's baseball owners are often heard saying the exact same thing. In order to prevent themselves from spending too much on players, the modern major-league owners have resorted to more and more desperate measures. They have tried to restrict free agency by setting up complicated compensation systems and by illegally colluding, or agreeing not to sign each other's free agents. In 1994, in order to accomplish the same end, they provoked a disastrous strike by the players' union that cut short the regular season and forced the cancellation of the playoffs and the World Series.

The 1879 NL owners passed a rule that allowed each team to "reserve" five of its top players each season. For that season the reserved players would be off-limits to other clubs. The clause worked, and it was gradually expanded. By 1883 clubs were allowed to reserve eleven players; by 1887 the reserve clause had become a fact of life for virtually every major-league player. With little competition for labor, salaries plummeted. If a team wished, it could renew any player's contract for another season simply by exercising the reserve clause. The following season it could renew the new contract, and so on. In effect, the reserve clause meant that a rookie who signed a one-year contract with a major-league club was bound to that club for the length of his career. If he did not like it, he could take up another profession; no other professional club would hire him. Perhaps the most outrageous thing about the reserve clause was that it worked in only one direction. If a team had no more use for a player because of injury or age—or for any other reason—it was free to release him on ten days' notice.

It was this aspect of the reserve clause that led a judge to rule, in a case brought by catcher Charlie Bennett, that the reserve clause was illegal and unenforceable. There were many other legal tests of the reserve clause during the late nineteenth-century, and the owners lost every single one. As late as 1914 a federal judge ruled that the reserve clause "lacked mutuality" and that "the ten-days clause gave first baseman Hal Chase the right to release *himself* from his contract with the Chicago White Sox on ten days" notice. Looking at the reserve clause's undistinguished record in the courts, it is difficult not to conclude that it may well have been illegal throughout its ninety-plus years of existence. According to a *Boston Globe* editorial from the 1880s, "It is generally accepted that baseball law is not legal law and could never be upheld in court, if that test should come." That test did not come for almost one hundred years. It was not until the 1970s that major-league players finally joined forces to drive the reserve clause out of baseball forever.

Interestingly, the reserve clause seems to have been more controversial in the authoritarian nineteenth-century than in the liberal, freedom-worshiping twentieth. For many nineteenth-century Americans, the reserve clause seemed like a kind of slavery. In 1887 New York Giants shortstop John Ward touched a national nerve by writing a celebrated magazine article entitled "Is the Base-Ball Player a Chattel [a piece of property]?" For others, however, the reserve clause was seen as essential in order to maintain stable professional baseball leagues. The American public's schizophrenic point of view on the reserve clause is captured by an 1889 editorial in the *St. Louis Globe-Democrat*, which thunders, "The reserve rule is, on paper, the most unfair and degrading measure . . . ever passed in a free country," before concluding, "still . . . it is necessary for the safety and preservation of the national game." Even most nineteenth-century major-league players conceded the fact that the reserve clause was good for the game, as long as the owners did not abuse the power it gave them. Unfortunately, the owners invariably took every opportunity to do just that.

Monopoly War I, the first of baseball's great economic wars, began with a letter sent by an obscure minor-league manager named Horace Phillips to Alfred Spink, the publisher of the St. Louis–based *Sporting News*, a weekly devoted largely to baseball. Phillips asked Spink's support for a proposed new major league to be based in various non-NL cities; he then invited baseball men from those cities to meet in Pittsburgh during the winter of 1880–1881. Even though Phillips was temporarily out of baseball—he returned to manage major-league teams in Pittsburgh for six seasons in the 1880s—by the time his idea came to fruition, he had gotten the ball rolling. Cincinnati, represented by baseball writer O. P. Caylor and brewery owner Justus Thorner, was the first city to respond.

Thorner was not the only brewer or whiskey maker to assist in the birth of the American Association, as the new league came to be called. The Louisville franchise was owned by J. H. Pank of the Kentucky Malting Company, and St. Louis was backed by Chris Von der Ahe, a flamboyant German saloonkeeper who had become interested in baseball, a contemporary observed, "as he might have become interested in pretzels, peanuts, or any other incitant to thirst and beer drinking." Men like these were not welcome in William Hulbert's NL. Cincinnati had been kicked out of the NL after the 1880 season for refusing to obey NL prohibitions against Sunday baseball and the selling of alcohol inside the ballpark. In most American communities these prohibitions were essential in order to market baseball to fans from the straitlaced middle classes, many of whom disapproved of drinking and subscribed to what was called the English Sunday—a Protestant custom that frowned upon any Sabbath activity more strenuous than a short walk. This kind of puritanism was foreign to the largely German-American fans of Cincinnati and St. Louis, whose culture had always allowed a little healthy outdoor fun on the Lord's day, and who considered beer as wholesome as mother's milk. Beer was also good business; historically, clubs in both cities had made as much or more profit from ballpark beer concessions than from ticket sales.

When the AA opened for business in 1882, it contained six franchises—Cincinnati, Philadelphia, Louisville, Pittsburgh, St. Louis, and Baltimore. The fact that the names on this list included some of the biggest and most lucrative baseball markets in the country makes the point that the AA was largely a creation of the NL's own restrictive and often high-handed policies. Louisville and St. Louis had dropped out of the NL in the aftermath of the gambling scandal of 1877. Cincinnati and Philadelphia were solid franchises that had been booted out of the NL for defying William Hulbert. Finally, markets as large as Baltimore and Pittsburgh had been left unexploited and open to the AA, while the NL preferred to keep franchises in decidedly minor-league towns like minuscule Troy, New York, and Worcester, Massachusetts. The bottom line was that deliberate actions by William Hulbert and the NL had opened the way for a second major league to come along and attack the NL's major-league monopoly. It did not have to happen. As would be the case in Monopoly Wars II, III, and IV, the major-league establishment had asked for Monopoly War I.

In the beginning there was no question of a peaceful relationship between the AA and the NL. The proud NL saw itself as the only major league, and it was convinced that America's fans felt the same way. William Hulbert gave himself a neck ache from looking down his nose at the new league. As he said in an 1882 newspaper interview:

> The League does not recognize the existence of any Association of ball clubs excepting itself and the League Alliance. . . I don't care to go into the question of the League's attitude toward the so-called American Association further than to say that it is not likely the League will be awake nights bothering its head about how to protect itself from a body in which it has no earthly interest, and which voluntarily assumed a position of hostility toward the League.[2]

The NL tried attacking the new league with propaganda, mocking everything from the AA's low twenty-five cent admission price—the NL held firm at fifty cents—to its colorful uniforms and Sunday games. The AA would be better named the "Beer and Whiskey League," NL supporters sneered.

Nearly all of these points, however, turned out to be strengths for the new league. Fans loved the AA's flashy style, low prices, and loose ballpark atmosphere. "Bringing baseball within reach of everybody's pocketbook" was the AA's advertising slogan. AA baseball may have been half-price, but it was far from cut-rate. Even though the majority of AA players had never played at the major-league level, AA clubs were able to turn up dozens of stars in the minor leagues and in amateur baseball.

The long list of future greats whose major-league debut came with the 1882 AA includes first baseman Charles Comiskey, slugger Pete Browning, second baseman Bid McPhee, and pitcher Guy Hecker. Hecker was an outstanding hitting pitcher in an era when many pitchers played right field on their off days. Hecker was good enough with the bat to play first base, normally a power hitter's position. Playing for Louisville in the pitcher's year of 1884, he set most of the AA's single-season pitching records, going 52-20 with a 1.80 ERA, completing 72 out of 73 starts, and racking up 670⅔ innings. He also hit .296 and led the team in home runs. McPhee played second base in Cincinnati for his entire eighteen-year major-league career. An amazing fielder who played bare-handed until the very end of his career, McPhee put up fielding numbers that still stack up with those of the greatest twentieth-century second basemen. Better known as the pinchpenny owner of the twentieth-century Chicago White Sox, as one of the founders of the American League, and as the man for whom Chicago's Comiskey Park was named, Charles Comiskey also had a long and glorious playing career. The top defensive first baseman of his day, Comiskey is often credited with being one of the first to play far off the bag and use the pitcher to cover first base on ground balls to the right side of the infield.

Many fans today see the name Pete Browning on the all-time career batting average list—he is number ten, at .343—and wonder who he was. During the 1880s, however, Browning, who played most of his career in his hometown of Louisville and was nick-named the "Louisville Slugger," was the most feared hitter in baseball. Standing over six feet tall and bulging with muscle, the right-handed Browning seemed like a giant to his contemporaries. Over his eleven-year career, he batted over .400 once, over .330 eight times, and over .300 eleven times. Playing in an era when home runs were scarce, he slugged over .500 four times. Browning's health and career were ultimately ruined by an undiagnosed ear infection called mastoiditis that affected his balance and ultimately led to brain damage; the constant pain of the disease drove him to alcoholism. Sadly, after his playing career, Browning—like many people in those days who suffered from hearing loss or other misunderstood physical problems—was committed to a mental hospital. He died in 1905 at the age of forty-four.

Pete Browning inadvertently created an enduring baseball legend when he commissioned an apprentice woodmaker named Bud Hillerich to make him a baseball bat. When other major-league hitters saw Browning hit, they wanted one of Hillerich's bats, too. So many orders for the "Louisville Slugger" bat came into Hillerich's shop that he went into the bat business full-time. That same Louisville company, now known as Hillerich and Bradsby, is still the world's top manufacturer of wooden bats, every one of which bears Pete Browning's nickname.

Stocked with young talent like Browning, McPhee, Hecker, and Comiskey, the AA as a whole drew more than twice as many fans as the NL in 1882. Five of the six original AA clubs actually outdrew Cap Anson's mighty White Stockings, who were reported to make two to three times as much money as any other NL team. The Philadelphia AA franchise alone was reported to have made a staggering profit of over $200,000 in its first year.

Not only did the new league exploit fertile new baseball markets and uncover new baseball talent but it also tapped into a previously neglected source of paying customers—the working class. The working class fan had always been given short shrift by the class-conscious NL. The late nineteenth-century was a time when a typical working-class breadwinner put in a punishing six-day workweek made up of ten-hour or even twelve-hour days. The NL's fifty-cent admission put their games financially out of reach for most working people, and so did its schedule. In most NL cities, games started thirty minutes to an hour after the close of local white-collar workers' office hours. The New York Stock Exchange, for example, closed at three o'clock, and baseball games started at three-thirty or four; in Chicago, the Board of Trade closed at one-thirty and the stock exchange at two, and baseball games began at three; in Washington, where government offices closed at four o'clock, games started at four-thirty, and of course there was no such thing as a night game in the 1880s. Because by Hulbert's edict no games were allowed on Sunday. NL games were effectively restricted to members of the middle and upper classes. The AA's Sunday games and low ticket prices made major-league baseball available to working-class fans for the first time since the NA days.

By 1883 the NL magnates realized that they had a fight on their hands from the new, fan-friendly working man's major league. They dropped weak sisters Worcester and Troy and added franchises in New York and Philadelphia. (Those clubs are the ancestors of today's San Francisco Giants and Philadelphia Phillies.) The NL also encouraged its clubs to ignore AA contracts and steal players from AA rosters at will. The AA responded by expanding in 1883, placing a franchise, the New York Metropolitans, into New York City and encouraging its clubs to raid NL rosters in return.

At this, the NL blinked and sued for peace. New NL president A. G. Mills—who had taken over for Arthur Soden, the man who had replaced William Hulbert after Hulbert's sudden death in 1882—counseled compromise. If the war continued, he warned, baseball risked "drifting in the direction which nearly ruined baseball many years ago, when contracts were disregarded and players were employed . . . without regard to the odium their past conduct had brought upon the game." There was plenty of money in baseball for everyone, Mills argued; all the owners had to do to make tremendous profits was to work together to keep the players down, so what was the point of owner fighting owner? Mills had a better idea. He proposed that the NL and AA unite and agree, along with as many minor leagues as were interested, to respect each other's markets, territories, and player contracts and to put an end to competitive bidding for players' services by expanding the reserve clause. AA clubs were allowed to continue selling alcohol and playing Sunday baseball.

In the spring of 1884 the two leagues agreed to Mills's plan and signed the Tripartite Agreement, also known as the National Agreement. This agreement, which marks the beginning of the vast professional structure that we now know as organized baseball, brought Monopoly War I to an end and put the expanded major-league monopoly on a rock-solid foundation. Just as they had in 1881, the owners had the players back under their thumb, and major-league baseball was once again a picture of peace, stability, and prosperity. Also as in 1881, on the outside looking in was a group of well-heeled men who wanted a piece of the major-league pie for themselves. A second monopoly war was just around the corner.

Monopoly War I could never have happened without William Hulbert's heavy-handed enforcement of his own rules and his stubborn unwillingness to admit franchises from large eastern cities. Monopoly War II would never have happened without the reserve clause. Bankrolled by an eccentric St. Louis streetcar developer and real estate baron named Henry Lucas, a new major league called the Union Association (UA) was formed in the fall of 1883. Besides Lucas, there were many other rich and prominent men involved with the UA. Brewer Adolphus Busch, a member of the family that makes Budweiser beer and owns today's St. Louis

Cardinals, invested in the UA; former star shortstop George Wright, part-owner of the Wright and Ditson Sporting Goods Company, a rival to Spalding's company, backed the new league, and provided the official UA baseball. Instead of putting franchises into neglected major markets, as the AA had done in 1882, the UA's primary strategy was to take the NL and the AA head on. UA franchises were placed in five AA cities—Baltimore, St. Louis, Cincinnati, Philadelphia, and Washington—and in three NL cities: Boston, Chicago, and Philadelphia. Before the 1884 season was over, the UA would also add clubs in Milwaukee, Saint Paul, Altoona, Wilmington, and Kansas City.

Where was the UA going to get enough talent to fill all of these rosters? The answer can be found in the UA constitution, which states that the UA would respect player contracts with other major leagues but would not honor the reserve clause, "which makes the player almost the slave of the club." The UA announced that it fully intended to ignore the reserve clause and offer a contract to any NL or AA player who had not signed a contract for the 1884 season. The NL and AA attacked the UA in a press campaign reminiscent of the NL's anti-AA rhetoric from 1882, stressing the "beer money" behind many UA franchises and the allegedly high number of "deadbeats and lushers" who were hired to play for UA teams. They even gave the UA an insulting nickname—the Onions. Lucas and his partners responded by attacking the morality of the reserve clause, hoping to win sympathy both from the major-league players and from the many fans who felt that the reserve clause was wrong.

NL President Mills took the UA threat very seriously. By March 1884, when it became apparent that the UA had signed dozens of reserved NL and AA stars, the two established major leagues voted to blacklist permanently any reserved player who jumped to the new league. As in the NL-AA conflict, all-out war followed, with both sides raiding each other's rosters aggressively. The NL and AA created a pool of money to be used to raise the pay of players who were considering jumping to the UA, and even stooped to hiring away players who were already under contract to the UA, something they had always maintained was immoral when the shoe was on the other foot. Ambidextrous pitching ace Tony "The Count" Mullane jumped from the AA to the UA, as did third baseman Jack Gleason and pitcher George Bradley. NL defectors included top-rank pitchers Tommy Bond, "One-Armed" Daily, Charlie Sweeney, Jim McCormick, Larry Corcoran, and Edward "The Only" Nolan; shortstop Jack Glasscock; and second baseman Fred "Sureshot" Dunlap. Mullane soon became the most prominent UA prize to jump back again after the AA dipped into its pool and offered Mullane a big raise to return to the fold and play for AA Toledo.

A secondary element of the major-league monopoly's defense strategy was to expand into potential UA markets before the UA could do so. Mills—shrewdly, as it turned out—suggested that the AA do the expanding, and so, when the 1884 season opened, the AA fielded new franchises in Toledo, Brooklyn, Indianapolis, and Washington (later replaced by Richmond).

With thirty-four different major-league clubs taking the field—there had been only sixteen in 1883—the 1884 season was a total mess. The NL lost its Cleveland franchise, which disbanded after losing Dunlap, McCormick, and three other starters to the UA; Providence, the eventual NL pennant-winner, nearly folded as well. With a finite amount of major-league talent spread very thin across the three leagues, dozens of teams became utterly noncompetitive. Six AA teams finished more than 27 games behind the first-place New York Metropolitans; four of those—Toledo, Richmond, Indianapolis, and Washington—did not return in 1885.

The UA pennant race was the biggest fiasco of all. St. Louis Maroons owner Henry Lucas, whose abundant wealth and energy were largely responsible for the existence of the UA, took advantage of those same qualities to build a powerhouse of a team that completely destroyed the competition. The Maroons played in the finest baseball facility in the league, a 10,000-seat palace called the Union Grounds. Managed by minor-league innovator Ted Sullivan, the Maroons grabbed the lion's share of the better NL and AA contract-jumpers, including Dunlap, who hit .412 to win the UA batting title; batting title runner-up Orator Shaffer, who hit .360; third baseman Jack Gleason; and pitchers Billy Taylor, who went 25-4 with a 1.68 ERA, and hard-throwing Charlie Sweeney, who went 24-7 with a 1.83 ERA. This team compiled an unbelievable record of 94 wins and 19 losses, finishing 21 games ahead of second-place Cincinnati and 61 games ahead of last-place Kansas City. Like the Boston Red Stockings of the 1870s, the Maroons were so good that they killed fan interest. Even in their hometown of St. Louis, fans preferred to pay to see the AA St. Louis Browns, who finished fourth and won 26 fewer games but were at least in a pennant race. The Maroons' dominance did not help attendance in the rest of the league, either. Ten UA teams finished thirty or more games out of the running; and six clubs dropped out before the season ended.

The 1884 season was a financial disaster, too. Both the NL and the AA suffered great losses, and Lucas and the UA lost a total of $250,000. It is not known how much Lucas lost personally in 1884, but a few years later he was found to be penniless and working as a clerk in a railroad ticket office. In any event, Lucas's short-term losses were enough to change his opinion of the reserve clause, which he had once termed "the most arbitrary and unjust rule ever suggested." In the fall of 1884 he sold out his players and the rest of the league, and accepted the NL's offer to admit the St. Louis Maroons into the NL to replace the moribund Cleveland franchise. On January 15, 1885, the Union Association formally went out of business. Lucas's entry into the NL camp did not go down easily with everyone on the winning side. Browns owner Von der Ahe was furious at having to share the St. Louis market with Lucas; he was placated only by the league's commitment never to allow the Maroons to play on Sunday. And NL president A. G. Mills, the general who had led the NL and AA to victory in Monopoly War II, resigned in protest after the NL and AA owners voted to rescind his blacklist edict and allow the UA contract-jumpers to return to the majors.

Notwithstanding all of the chaos, bitterness, and ill will of Monopoly Wars I and II, the middle 1880s was a time of tremendous innovation and experimentation in baseball. Competition—something the major-league monopoly had always tried to stifle—led to the tapping of new markets, the use of new marketing techniques, and many other improvements in the game. Major-league attendance skyrocketed as more and more clubs built first-class ballparks on the model of Chicago's Lakefront Park and St. Louis's ultramodern Union Grounds. Many of the game's stars became national figures; they appeared on the increasingly popular tobacco cards—the forerunners of today's bubble gum cards—and toured with vaudeville companies in the off-season. Cap Anson, King Kelly, John Ward, and Arlie Latham were just a few of the popular baseball stars of the 1880s who appeared on the vaudeville stage, the nineteenth-century equivalent of the movies. The ubiquitous Ted Sullivan and others pioneered the idea of special ballpark promotions, including doubleheaders

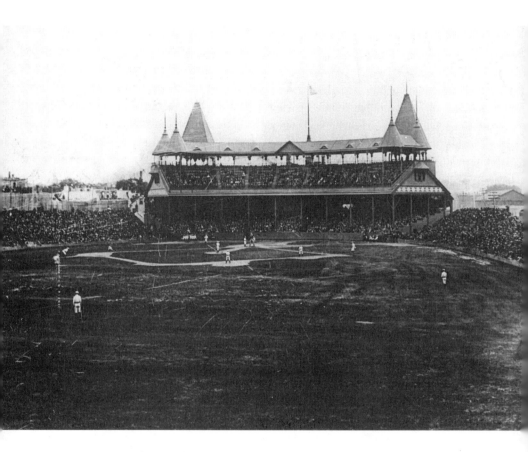

The Walpole Street Grounds, home park of
the NL Boston Red Stockings of the 1870s and
the NL Boston Beaneaters

and ladies' days. Overall, more and more women fans were drawn into baseball. Sullivan also popularized the use of the term "fan"—short for "fanatic"—to refer to baseball fans; previously, baseball fans had been known as "cranks."

Gloves were improved upon and became generally used by the end of the decade. Pitching rules underwent the most drastic changes. In 1883 pitchers could not throw with their arm higher than the shoulder; batters could call for a pitch to be thrown to either a high or a low strike zone, and it took seven balls to earn a base on balls. Four years later, in 1887, pitchers could throw overhand; there was only one strike zone, and five balls were required for a base on balls. During the 1880s, many other changes were made in the rules governing pitchers' motions, their deliveries, and the pitching distance from home plate. The tremendous demand for playing talent led many minor-league clubs to sign African-American players, in violation of the color line—a long-standing baseball tradition going back to the days of the NABBP. In 1884 the AA Toledo club used African-American catcher Fleet Walker and, for a few games, his brother Welday, an outfielder. The Walkers were the last African-Americans knowingly accepted into the major leagues until Jackie Robinson played for the Brooklyn Dodgers in 1947.

CHAPTER
FIVE

$\mathscr{W}$inner Take All:
The Forgotten World Series
of the 1880s

One of the more lasting baseball innovations of the
nineteenth century came about in 1882 when the winner
of the NL pennant met the winner of the AA pennant in
a postseason exhibition series. In a sense, this was the
first World Series. The two pennant winners met again
in 1884; soon these series developed into an annual
event. The idea of two major-league pennant-winners
playing a postseason World Series was so popular
among fans in the 1880s that it was resurrected soon
after baseball returned to a two-major-league format in
1903. With the exceptions of 1904 and 1994, the
World Series has been played every year from then until
today. It is America's most prestigious sporting event.
The amazing thing about the World Series is that the
major-league owners stumbled upon the idea more or
less by accident.

In the beginning, of course, the NL did not want
another major league; and after the AA came along, the
AA did not want to play a postseason championship
series. The World Series began when, ignoring the state

of war that existed between their two leagues, the AA champion Cincinnati Reds and the NL champion Chicago White Stockings agreed between themselves to play a best-three-games-out-of-five series in October of 1882. Even though this series was no grand national event along the lines of the AL-NL World Series of later times, it was the first time that two major-league pennant-winners had met, and it was sold to the public as deciding the "baseball championship of the world." Because AA president Denny McKnight had specifically forbidden the 1882 Reds to play any kind of postseason series with Chicago, Cincinnati came up with the cute trick of releasing its entire roster just before the series was to begin; they signed the players to what was technically a new team the following day. The series was tied at one game apiece when a furious McKnight telegraphed Reds player-manager Dick Fulmer that he would ban the entire team from the AA forever if they went through with game three. That was the end of the first World Series.

The next year the NL attempted to embarrass the AA by challenging it to play another World Series, knowing the AA would refuse. The AA made no reply. But it was a different story in 1884. The AA and NL had made peace and signed the National Agreement; part of that agreement specifically granted permission for the NL and AA pennant-winners to schedule a postseason World Series. For the next seven years, World Series were held. These series did not always measure up to the consistent excitement and high drama of the twentieth-century World Series. There were terrible low points, like the inconclusive 1885 series and the 1890 series between Louisville and Brooklyn, which had to be called off for lack of interest. Like the World Series of today, however, at their best the World Series of the 1880s provided fans with thrilling moments and served as a national showcase for many of the game's greatest stars.

Representing the NL in 1884 were the Providence Grays. The Grays were a solid team that had won the 1879 pennant under George Wright and finished second to Cap Anson's White Stockings in 1880, 1881, and 1882. They were managed by Frank Bancroft, a pioneer executive and one of the rare managers of the time who was not an active or former professional player.

Like Ted Sullivan, Bancroft made an extremely underrated contribution to the early development of baseball. A Civil War veteran, he operated his first baseball team as a sideline to his hotel business in New Bedford, Massachusetts. A fiery competitor who did not suffer foolish owners gladly, Bancroft went on to manage, Billy Martin–like, seven different major-league teams between 1880 and 1902. Bancroft stands at the head of a line of famous mentor-pupil relationships that continues to this day: his protégé, Detroit center fielder Ned Hanlon, managed the great Orioles teams of the 1890s; Hanlon taught third baseman John McGraw, who went on manage the New York Giants in the 1900s, 1910s, and 1920s; McGraw's protégé, outfielder Casey Stengel, managed the great Yankees dynasty of the 1950s and 1960s; his protégé, Billy Martin, became one of the greatest managers of the 1970s and 1980s. The fire lit by Frank Bancroft is still burning bright today. Two players who learned their baseball under Billy Martin—Mike Hargrove and Lou Piniella—are currently managing in the major leagues; Chris Chambliss or Willie Randolph may soon make it three.

An innovator in many ways, Bancroft sponsored the first visit by an American professional team to the Caribbean when he took his Worcester club to Havana, Cuba, in 1879. He returned many times with major-league teams and helped guide the early development of Cuban baseball. Bancroft also had a sharp eye for talent and discovered an amazing number of nineteenth-century stars, including Art Irwin, Tim Keefe, Harry Stovey, and John Lee Richmond. He was still working in the Cincinnati Reds front office when he died after a long illness in 1921 at the age of seventy-four. Bedridden throughout the Black Sox scandal, which broke in late 1920, Bancroft never learned that his beloved Reds had been given their 1919 World Series victory by a dishonest White Sox team that was playing to lose. Friends and family kept him from hearing the news.

Playing first base for Providence was the ageless Joe "Old Reliable" Start, whose career spanned twenty-eight years; Start played in his rookie season against pre–Civil War great Jim Creighton; he retired in 1886 at age forty-three. Also appearing in the 1884 Providence lineup were third baseman Jeremiah Denny, who in the early 1890s became the last major-league position player to play bare-handed, and perennial .300-hitter Paul Hines. Nevertheless Jim Mutrie's AA-champion New York Mets were heavy favorites. There is no question that they were the superior offensive team. Led by third baseman Dude Esterbrook and slugging first baseman Dave Orr, who batted .354 and hit nine home runs, the Mets played 107 games and scored 734 runs, 69 more than Providence scored in 112 games.

Eighteen eighty-four, however, was a pitcher's year. The main reason for this was a rule change that removed all restrictions on the pitcher's arm angle; previously pitchers could pitch no higher than sidearm. Immediately after the rule change, three things happened: pitchers began to throw more and more overhand, runs became harder and harder to come by, and the number of sore arms increased astronomically. The overall National League ERA dropped from 3.13 to 2.98; four starting pitchers, as well as the entire Providence staff, recorded ERAs below 2.00. In the AA, Louisville's Guy Hecker won the ERA title at 1.80; the two-man New York staff of Tim Keefe and Jack Lynch won 37 games apiece and allowed the fewest runs of any contending club.

Paradoxically, the greatest pitching performance in the pitcher's year of 1884 was turned in by Providence's Charles "Old Hoss" Radbourn. Radbourn was a throwback; throughout his career, he kept the same submarine delivery that had been in vogue since the National Association days. Old Hoss was a hard thrower, in spite of his five-foot-nine-inch, 168-pound frame, but he did not try to overpower every hitter. He owed both his success and his famous endurance in large part to a deceptive change-up. Radbourn had joined the Grays in 1881 as a backup to early pitching great John Ward, but as Ward's arm began to give out, Radbourn assumed more and more of the team's pitching duties. Radbourn won 25, 31, and 49 games respectively from 1881 to 1883, and lowered his ERA from 2.43 to 2.09 to 2.05. Early on in the 1884 season, however, Bancroft benched Radbourn in favor of a twenty-year-old phenom from California named Charlie Sweeney. Sweeney was an overhand fastballer who struck out an astonishing nineteen Buffalo Bisons in one game on June 7.

Invariably photographed wearing a menacing scowl, Radbourn was tough, bad-tempered, and belligerent; he was the kind of guy who liked to give the finger to the camera in the team photo. He did not handle his return to backup status very well at all. He sulked, openly criticized Sweeney, and when he did pitch, intentionally crossed up his catcher so often that Bancroft had to suspend him.

Fortunately for Radbourn, Sweeney possessed one quality that Frank Bancroft disliked even more than Radbourn's childish antics: he drank too much. Sweeney's drinking got worse and worse as the season wore on. Finally, in late July, when Bancroft caught a

WHEN WHISKEY THREATENED

*A newspaper cartoon depicts major-league baseball's
losing battle against alcoholism.*

tanked-up Sweeney drinking whiskey between innings
of a game in which he was pitching, the two got into a
shouting match and Sweeney walked out on the team.
Because contemporary rules forbade player substitutions except for illness or injury, the Grays had to finish
the game with only eight men. Given back his starting

pitcher's job, a jubilant Radbourn publicly vowed to deliver the pennant to Providence.

As for Sweeney, if his drinking in any way hurt his pitching, it is hard to tell from his 1884 statistics. He was 17-8 when he left Providence. Expelled from the NL after his run-in with Bancroft, Sweeney caught on with Henry Lucas's St. Louis Maroons and led them to the UA pennant with a record of 24-7 and an ERA of 1.83. Old Hoss Radbourn pitched even better. He made good on his promise by having the season of his life, starting 73 games and finishing all but two. Taking the ball nearly every day, he pitched a league-leading 678.2 innings—four outs shy of the all-time single-season record for most innings pitched. His won-lost record was 60-12; he had an ERA of 1.38.

For most of the 1884 season, Providence and Boston ran neck and neck; the two archrivals seemed to have exhausted each other on June 6, when Radbourn and Boston's Jumbo Jim Whitney pitched to a grueling 1–1 sixteen-inning deadlock. The two clubs traded first and second place on an almost daily basis until August 7, when Radbourn got a second wind and reeled off 18 wins in a row. Before they knew what had hit them, the Red Stockings found themselves 10½ games out. As for Sweeney, his drinking did catch up with him in the end. In 1894 he shot and killed a man during a drunken melee in a San Francisco saloon. He was sentenced to ten years in San Quentin prison, but died of tuberculosis in 1902 at the age of thirty-nine.

When the Providence Grays arrived at New York City's original Polo Grounds, located just north of Manhattan's Central Park, to play the first three games of the best-three-games-out-of-five World Series on October 23, 24, and 25, Old Hoss Radbourn was still on a roll. Even though the bookmakers liked the Mets, New York fans seemed to sense impending disaster; together, the three games drew a total of only 3,100 fans. Radbourn easily out dueled the Mets' Keefe to win games one and two, allowing the New York hitters a total of only seven hits and three runs. Things only got worse for the Mets in game three. Radbourn and the Grays were nine runs ahead when Keefe—who, strangely enough, was serving as umpire on his off-day—spared his teammates further humiliation by calling the game "on account of darkness," in spite of the fact that the sun was shining brightly. The Grays had won the series, three games to none.

Not surprisingly, Old Hoss Radbourn's arm never entirely recovered from pitching 1,311 innings combined in 1883 and 1884. He won twenty games five more times, but his seasonal ERAs rose steadily and his workload dropped each year. Radbourn's arm was said to be so bad later in his career that he was unable to comb his own hair. In a 1908 interview, Radbourn's manager with the 1884 Grays, Frank Bancroft, remembered the painful ritual that Radbourn had to go through before each start: "[He went] out to the ballpark hours before the rest of the team and [began] to warm up by throwing a few feet and increasing the distance until he could finally throw the ball from the outfield to home plate. The players, all eagerness to win, would watch "Rad," and when he would succeed in making his customary long-distance throw they would look at one another and say the Old Hoss is ready and we can't be beat."[1] After going 12-12 with a 4.25 ERA for Cincinnati in 1891, Radbourn retired with a career won-lost record of 308-191. He was a member of the first class of players elected to the Hall of Fame in 1939.

In 1885, for the first time, the World Series attracted serious national attention. Part of the reason was the matchup of Cap Anson's Chicago White Stockings and Charles Comiskey's St. Louis Browns. The White Stockings were coming off the fourth of their five NL pennants; the Browns had won their first of four straight

AA pennants. Besides being the two greatest dynasties of the decade, the Browns and White Stockings had a great deal else in common: both were psychologically and physically aggressive teams that intimidated umpires as well as opponents; both were led by brilliant player-manager first basemen; and both played a hustling, base-stealing, extra-base-taking style of baseball.

All similarities between the two champion teams end with their owners. It is doubtful that any pair of nineteenth-century baseball men could have been more different than Albert Spalding and Chris Von der Ahe. A former star ballplayer, Spalding was a midwestern WASP who was tight with a dollar. Spalding was a classic Victorian, for whom business success was a vehicle for achieving social status and respectability. This explains his repeated involvement in baseball tours to England; what Spalding and many other American baseball entrepreneurs wanted more than anything was the approval of the English, who were the world's premier sportsmen as well as the masters of the world's greatest colonial empire.

Spalding's concern with middle-class respectability also explains his fanatical concern with drinking. Besides sharing William Hulbert's disdain for Sunday baseball and the selling of beer in ballparks, Spalding would, from time to time, force his White Stockings to sign public pledges not to drink alcohol during the season. In 1887 Spalding announced to all decent Chicagoans that "our men this year do not drink, and they take pride in keeping up the reputation of the club. . . . We shall no longer endure the criticism of respectable people because of drunkenness in the Chicago nine."[2] It is hard to think of George Gore or King Kelly signing such a pledge without, at the very least, cracking a smile. Spalding never let reality get in the way of his campaign to liberate Anson's boys from the negative effects of drink. He became fascinated with all sorts of quackish theories about how to rid the body of alcohol; one of the benefits of spring training in Hot Springs, Arkansas, Spalding maintained, was that soaking in hot water would "boil out all the alcoholic microbes which have impregnated the system of these men during the winter."

Chris Von der Ahe, on the other hand, was a free-spending, hard-partying, flashy-dressing German immigrant who could not have cared less about Spalding's kind of respectability. A successful saloon owner who invested in baseball in order to be able to sell beer to baseball fans, the only thing Von der Ahe knew about America's national pastime was that it made people thirsty to sit in the sun and watch it. A hero to largely German-American St. Louis for returning the city to major-league status in 1882, Von der Ahe was in many ways a sort of nineteenth-century George Steinbrenner. He loved public attention and frequently accompanied the Browns on road trips, marching proudly ahead of his men as they made the walk from their team hotel to the ballpark. He referred to himself as "der boss president." If there had been such a thing as a team media guide in the 1880s, Von der Ahe undoubtedly would have put his own picture on the cover.

Von der Ahe lurched unpredictably between utter indulgence and petty harassment of his ballplayers. On one hand, he paid the highest salaries in baseball. After one season Von der Ahe was so happy with the performance of his Browns that he built a row of apartment buildings and named each building after one of his players. On the other hand, when he did not like the way the team was playing, he would relieve his frustration by fining his players for such offenses as singing or "acting up" during games. He was also fond of delivering ridiculous pep talks to his team, as in 1885, when he told them: "See here now, I want you to stop all this slushing around and play ball. If you win the championship, I give you a new suit of clothes. If you don't, you will have to eat snowballs all winter." Von der Ahe once spent $20,000 to rent a special luxury train to take his team from St. Louis to New York City in style. In a fit of pique after losing the 1888 World Series to Detroit, Von der Ahe sold five of his biggest stars to other teams for a total of $15,000.

Unlike Steinbrenner, however, Von der Ahe seems to have had some awareness of his own limitations as a baseball man. He backed to the hilt, financially and morally, both manager Ted Sullivan, who built the team from the ground up, and Sullivan's protégé and successor Charles Comiskey. According to G. W. Axelson's 1919 biography of Comiskey, *Commy*, Von der Ahe raised Comiskey's salary from $90 a month to $8,000 a year over the course of his seven years as St. Louis manager. The result was the St. Louis Browns of 1885–1888, who completely dominated the rest of the AA and who may well have deserved the nickname "the best team on earth."

At first base for Von der Ahe's Browns was Comiskey, who was a good hitter, though not in Anson's class. As a manager, Comiskey was feared, both as a tactician and as an acid-tongued abuser of umpires, as much or more than Cap Anson. "I believe that kicking is half the game," Comiskey once told a reporter.

At third base was Arlie Latham, known as "The Freshest Man on Earth," after a song that he sang in a popular vaudeville show. Latham had little power, but he was a terrific defensive third baseman and a smart, hustling player who sparked the Browns' offense with his hyperaggressive base stealing. A favorite with the fans, he was also one of baseball's pioneer bench jockeys. On the pretext of serving as the first or third base coach, Latham would roam up and down the baselines, stealing the opposition's signs and unnerving pitchers and catchers with a nonstop stream of insults and abuse. Responsibility for the rule restricting base coaches to coaching boxes has been attributed both to Latham and to Anson. New York Giants manager John McGraw thought so highly of Latham that, in 1909, he made him baseball's first full-time paid coach. Latham also got into four games that year and became, at forty-nine, the oldest major-league player ever to steal a base.

The heart of the St. Louis offense was the speedy outfield trio of Curt Welch, Tip O'Neill, and Tommy McCarthy. Welch was a superb center fielder who played daringly shallow; a mediocre hitter, he worked at getting on base by drawing walks and getting hit by pitches. McCarthy was a smart player, who after leaving St. Louis served as player-manager of the Boston Beaneaters, the great NL dynasty of the 1890s. Canadian-born Tip O'Neill was one of the greatest sluggers of the 1880s; he batted third in the Browns lineup. A converted pitcher, O'Neill batted .350 in 1885, his first full season as an outfielder. He went on to hit .326 lifetime and won two batting titles. His finest season came in 1887, when hitters' statistics were inflated by rules and scoring changes that required four strikes for a strikeout and counted walks as hits. O'Neill's 1887 stats are impressive anyway: he batted .492 (.435 without the walks), slugged .691, and collected 225 hits, 52 doubles, 19 triples, and 14 home runs—all league-leading figures.

The heart of the St. Louis defense was a magnificent pitching staff of right-handed sidearmers Davy Foutz, who led the AA in 1886 with 41 wins and a 2.11 ERA, and "Parisian" Bob Caruthers—so-called because he had once traveled to Paris, France, during a contract holdout—who led the AA in 1885 with 40 wins and an ERA of 2.07. In the late 1880s the Browns added Charles "Silver" King. King was a brilliant right-hander with an extreme crossfire-type delivery, who went 45-21 with a 1.64 ERA in 1888. A proud and capable man,

King became one of a number of major-league players to quit baseball in mid-career during the 1890s, when baseball owners artificially lowered players' salaries. At twenty-nine, he started a construction business and became so successful that he was able to retire a wealthy man in his fifties.

The 1885 World Series should have been a classic. In order to take advantage of what was expected to be extraordinary nationwide interest, plans were made to play a seven-game series, with games to be held in Chicago, St. Louis, Pittsburgh, and Cincinnati. The excitement had reached a fever pitch when the two teams paraded in open horse-drawn carriages to the Chicago ballpark for game one. Von der Ahe spared no expense, outfitting his team's carriage horses with brown blankets that read "St. Louis Browns, Champions American Association." He also hired a special train, decorated with pro–St. Louis banners, to bring thousands of Browns rooters to the game.

Unfortunately, the games themselves were a big disappointment. Game one was an error-filled fiasco that was called because of darkness, with the score tied. The series ended the same way—tied 3-3-1—because both teams claimed victory in game two. In that game the White Stockings scored three runs in the sixth inning to take a 5–4 lead. Browns manager Comiskey was livid, because Chicago's go-ahead rally had been aided by what he saw as a bad call on the bases by umpire Dan Sullivan. St. Louis fans were raining insults down on Sullivan. "Crook! Train robber! Jesse James!" they shouted, as Comiskey came over to argue. "Your people are horse thieves," he screamed at Sullivan, "and if you don't change that decision, I'll take my team off the field." When the umpire refused to budge, Comiskey followed through on his threat. Even though the game was ruled a Chicago victory by forfeit, the Browns always insisted that they had won the game and the series, 4–2.

Chris Von der Ahe, the George Steinbrenner of the 1880s

There was still plenty of bitterness left over from this episode the following year, when both teams repeated as champions. Spalding declared that he wanted nothing to do with "that man, Von der Ahe." When Von der Ahe sent Comiskey to personally challenge Anson to a rematch after the 1886 season, Anson replied, on Spalding's instructions, that Chicago would play on only one condition: "winner take all"—in other words, the winning team would receive every penny of the World Series gate from every game. To everyone's shock, Von der Ahe accepted these terms, telling Comiskey in his thick German accent; "I know your boys can lick the tails off them Chicagos."

By far the best World Series of the 1880s, the 1886 best-four-of-seven matchup between Chicago and St. Louis was decided by what is probably the only play in baseball that can top a seventh-game bottom-of-the-ninth homer à la Bill Mazeroski. Would you believe an extra-inning World Series–winning steal of home plate?

The stakes were high in the 1886 series in more ways than one. Both teams had something to prove. The proud Chicago White Stockings wanted to back up their frequent boasts that the National League was superior to the upstart American Association. Like Joe Namath's 1969 New York Jets, the 1886 St. Louis Browns carried the burden of having to win legitimacy for an entire league. There was also the personal animosity, dating back to the disputed 1885 series, between managers Anson and Comiskey. Finally, there was the added interest of the winner-take-all format. Most of the White Stockings and Browns had already hedged their bets by secretly pairing off with a member of the opposition and promising to split their winnings fifty-fifty. The fans knew nothing about this, however, and they came out to the ballpark in droves. The seven games drew between 5,000 and 10,000 fans each, easily the largest attendance of any World Series of the 1880s.

The first three games were played in Chicago, where the White Stockings and their ace pitcher John Clarkson enjoyed a huge home-field advantage. St. Louis was lucky to get out of town with a record of 1-2. Taking advantage of their own home cooking, familiar ballpark, and rowdy, leather-lunged fans— St. Louis was an umpire's nightmare—the Browns beat Clarkson 8–5 behind Davy Foutz, and banged out eleven hits the next day to win 10–3.

Game six matched the two staff aces—Clarkson for Chicago and Caruthers for St. Louis. Leading 3–0 after seven innings, the White Stockings seemed well on their way to tying the series and forcing a game seven. But the Browns rallied for three runs in the bottom of the eighth. The score remained tied 3–3 going into the bottom of the tenth of the first extra-inning game in World Series history.

St. Louis's Curt Welch led off the inning. Determined to get on base any way he could, Welch leaned into a Clarkson pitch, dropped his bat, and began to jog to first base. Umpire Dickey Pearce—the same Dickey Pearce who had played shortstop for the legendary Brooklyn Atlantics of the 1860s—ruled that Welch had let the ball hit him intentionally, and ordered him back to the plate. Welch then singled. He advanced to second base on an error, and to third on a sacrifice bunt by second baseman Yank Robinson. Normally, it would have been child's play for the fundamentally sound Browns to score the winning run from third with one out. Next up, however, was Doc Bushong, who was a fine defensive catcher but easily the worst hitter on the team. The right-handed Bushong routinely batted two or even three places below the Browns' pitcher in the batting order and struggled to keep his batting average above .200. A pinchhitter was out of the question; not until three years later was a manager allowed to substitute for one of his players, except in case of injury.

Welch and Comiskey did have an idea, though. As Comiskey told biographer Axelson years later:

> In order to worry Clarkson, who was pitching, Welch took a long lead off third, too long in fact, for which I was partially responsible as I was coaching. On the first ball pitched Welch was so far away from the bag that Mike [King] Kelly, who was catching, could have nailed him easily. Bushong had let it go without offering to swing at it. It was then that Welch showed his usual brainwork. Curt figured that if he kept at the same risky distance from the bag Kelly would signal for a high ball on the inside in order to have the advantage of a quick throw to Burns [the third baseman]. It turned out just like that. Clarkson burned one by Bushong's shirt and Kelly in his eagerness to get the ball away to catch Welch slightly fumbled it and it rolled about ten feet. Welch must have divined the fumble, for he was off like a flash toward home plate. Never in my life, I believe, have I seen a man go so fast. He seemed to skim over the ground.[3]

Welch executed a brilliant hook slide and crossed the plate safely underneath Kelly's desperate diving tag. Because the gate receipts for the 1886 series came to approximately $15,000, Welch's feat has gone down in baseball history as the "$15,000 slide." Even though, as it was discovered later, most of the St. Louis players split their winnings with members of the White Stockings, many of Anson's men were reported to have bet so heavily on themselves with St. Louis bookies that Chris Von der Ahe had to pay their train fare home.

Some historians argue that the 1880s postseason series were mere informal exhibitions that do not deserve the name World Series. It is a measure of how seriously they were taken at the time, however, that the 1880s series began—like modern World Series—to produce scapegoats as well as heroes. After Chicago's heartbreaking loss in 1886, White Stockings owner Al Spalding traded pitcher Jim McCormick and outfielder Abner Dalrymple, both of whom had played poorly against the St. Louis Browns.

The following year it was Chris Von der Ahe's turn to be disappointed. The opposing team was the Detroit Wolverines, whose fearsome lineup of sluggers had batted .299 as a team and scored 969 runs in 124 games, by far the most in the NL. Detroit had the NL batting champ, Sam Thompson, who drove in an incredible 166 runs, and the NL's three top run scorers: first baseman Dan Brouthers at 153, shortstop Jack Rowe at 135, and infielder Hardie Richardson at 131. Rounding out the Detroit lineup were ex–Union Association star Fred Dunlap and catcher Charlie Bennett. The pitching staff was anchored by Charles "Lady" Baldwin and Charles "Pretzels" Getzien. Pejorative and ethnic nicknames were common in the 1880s; many German-American players had to put up with being called "Pretzels" or "Pickles." Poor Baldwin's nickname has been explained either as a play on his middle name, Busted, or as a mocking reference to the fact that he did not drink, smoke, or swear. Detroit owner Frederick Stearns earned the 1887 pennant the old-fashioned way—he bought it. Spending a reported $25,000 over three years, Stearns bought an entire minor-league team in order to get Thompson, and paid cash for the heart of the powerful Buffalo lineup: Brouthers, Deacon White, Richardson, and Rowe.

Still, St. Louis fans were optimistic; even though their lineup included only one slugger who matched up with Thompson, Brouthers, and Rowe—Tip O'Neill— they had, in fact, scored more runs than Detroit during the regular season: 1,131. As the series approached, the Browns boasted publicly that they would be able to run on Detroit catcher Bennett, who was playing with severe hand and finger injuries.

After the great success of the 1886 series, the 1887 edition was expanded and turned into a fifteen-game ten-city national tour. This was too much of a good thing for the fans; the final two games drew a total of only 1,030 people. By then Detroit had already beaten the Browns, thoroughly outhitting, outpitching, and even outrunning Von der Ahe's speedsters. Inspired by predictions that the Browns would run wild, Charlie Bennett caught nearly every game and held team spark-plug Arlie Latham to a single stolen base. Detroit won the series in a rout, ten games to five. That winter, a furious Von der Ahe sold fan favorites Caruthers, Foutz, and Bushong to Brooklyn, and Welch and shortstop Jack Gleason to the Philadelphia Athletics. These deals were about as popular among the people of St. Louis as near beer; it was months before Von der Ahe dared to be seen in public.

The 1888 World Series was notable for the first appearance by a New York team, Jim Mutrie's New York Giants. The Giants featured slugging first baseman Roger Connor, pitcher-turned-shortstop John Ward, outfielder Orator O'Rourke, catcher Buck Ewing, and pitchers Tim Keefe and Mickey Welch. All six of these men are now in the Hall of Fame. Keefe carried the Giants through the pennant race, going 35-12 with a league-leading 1.74 ERA, and single-handedly took the World Series from a jerry-built St. Louis Browns team by going 4-0 and allowing only 19 hits in 36 innings. He defeated St. Louis ace Silver King three times.

The Giants repeated in 1889 and played Brooklyn in what would have been the first subway series—if the New York City subway system had been built at that time. To New York–area fans, however, this series was not a first; even as far back as 1889 the two cities on the East River considered themselves ancient baseball enemies. Recalling the inter-city all-star contests of the 1850s and 1860s, *The New York Times* wrote: "The rivalry between New York and Brooklyn as regards baseball is unparalleled in the history of the national game." The outcome of the 1889 series eerily foreshadowed later Yankee-Dodger matchups of the 1940s and 1950s. Led by ex-Browns Caruthers and Foutz, Brooklyn won the first three games of the best-five-of-nine series to raise its fans' hopes sky high, before dropping five in a row and losing the series five games to three.

For all of its ups and downs, by the late 1880s the World Series had become part of major-league baseball tradition. Like the modern World Series, it was something that fans eagerly looked forward to at the end of the regular season, the way children, after a big meal, look forward to dessert. The 1890 World Series, however, was the last nineteenth-century postseason series to be played under the popular two-league World Series format.

What killed off the World Series 1880s-style? The answer is the return of the monopoly wars. Disgusted with the owners' abuse of the reserve clause, in 1890 the players broke away and formed their own major league, the Players League (PL). Once again there were three major leagues; once again there was war. With most of the better players having gone over to the PL, the NL was seriously weakened. It was even worse in the AA, where many teams were manned by minor-league talent at best. At the end of the season, King Kelly's Boston club, the champions of the best league in baseball—the Players League—were not even invited to the World Series. Instead, the series was played by NL Brooklyn, a mediocre team that had remained relatively unscathed by defections to the PL, and the AA champs, an utterly faceless Louisville club with few players that any fans outside of Kentucky knew or cared anything about.

The fans had already voted with their feet in Monopoly War III by abandoning the two established major leagues in droves and flocking to PL parks during the regular season. There was little interest in a matchup of the NL and AA pennant-winners. After several delays caused by rain, and crowds of 1,000, 600, and 300 for games five through seven, the dreary 1890 World Series was put out of its misery. Fittingly, nobody won. The final result was Brooklyn three games, Louisville three games, and one tie.

CHAPTER SIX

Dewdrops and Thunderbolts: Nineteenth-Century Pitching

Sportswriters and fans like to think of baseball as a game that never changes, that the basics of baseball—four balls and three strikes, 60 feet 6 inches from home plate to the mound, fastballs and curves—have stayed the same for as long as there has been baseball.

But have they? When you take a closer look, you see that the real story of baseball is one of almost constant change. The balance of power between pitcher and hitter, which determines more than anything else how many runs are scored in a game, is very delicate and changeable. It shifts back and forth from season to season, so that some years are pitchers' years and others are hitters' years. The balance can be drastically affected by changes in the rules governing, say, the height of the mound, the style of the pitchers' deliveries, and the size of the strike zone, as well as by things that are harder to control, such as the advent of new pitches, accidental changes in the manufacture of baseballs, and even the weather.

Because this balance never stops changing and evolving, baseball has to keep fine-tuning and tinkering with its rules in order to keep the number of runs scored within traditional limits. The process is a little like the making of blended whiskey or fine cigars; because the ingredients change unpredictably from year to year, the art of the master blender comes in adjusting the mixture so that the end result tastes the same as last year's product.

Sometimes, as in the home run explosion of 1987, a sudden shift in the balance between hitting and pitching is caused by factors that are never explained. Other times, the balance is changed on purpose. A good example of this occurred in the late 1960s. Starting around 1964, for no apparent reason, pitchers in both leagues gradually began to get the upper hand in their battle with major-league hitters. By 1968 the overall NL batting average had fallen to .243, the lowest figure since 1908. The AL batting average had fallen to .230, the lowest it had ever been in the league's sixty-nine-year history. Pitcher Bob Gibson of the St. Louis Cardinals recorded a microscopic ERA of 1.12; over in the AL, Luis Tiant of the Cleveland Indians had an ERA of 1.60, and Sam McDowell, Dave McNally, Denny McClain, and Tommy John all were under 2.00. McClain went 31-6 to become the last man in baseball history to win 30 games. Boston's Carl Yastrzemski won the AL batting title with an average of only .301; he was the only hitter in the league to bat over .290.

Major-league baseball officials decided that the hitters needed help. They reduced the slope of the pitching mound and lowered its height by five inches. The results were dramatic. League batting averages shot up to .250 in the NL and .246 in the AL. Bob Gibson's ERA rose more than a full run, to 2.18, and NL runs scored increased by 15 percent. No pitcher in either league recorded an ERA lower than 2.10. Minnesota's Rod Carew won the AL batting title with an average of .332.

What happened in 1968 was not really very unusual. Several times in this century, the major leagues have openly and intentionally altered the rule book in order to raise or lower the number of runs scored.

All of the changes of the twentieth century, however, are nothing compared to what major leaguers of the nineteenth century had to live through. The last quarter of the nineteenth century, particularly the decade of the 1880s, was a time of rapid, almost chaotic change in the rules, particularly those governing pitching. Many rules changed almost on a yearly basis. The game was still very young, and baseball was groping in the dark, trying, often by simple trial and error, to find the right balance between offense and defense, and to learn how to maintain that balance in the face of the tremendous changes that were taking place in every other facet of the game.

Take a look at one example: the rule governing how many balls were required for a base on balls. In 1876 it took nine balls to draw a walk; in practice, though, it took twenty-seven, because the umpire would only call every third one. In 1879 the number was still nine, but now all balls were called. In 1880 the number was reduced to eight; in 1884, to six; in 1886, back up to seven; and in 1887, down to five. Finally, in 1889, four balls were settled upon.

Today's players often have great difficulty adjusting to very slight changes in, say, the strike zone or the balk rule. It is hard to imagine how modern hitters, many of whom use the base on balls as an important weapon in their arsenal, would have handled playing in the nineteenth century. Undoubtedly, Rickey Henderson, Wade Boggs, and Frank Thomas would have spent much of the 1880s talking to themselves.

A similar list of year-by-year changes could be made for the size of the pitcher's box and the distance from the pitcher to home plate. All of these things were in a state of flux from the birth of the NL in 1876 until 1893. A less confusing way of understanding those years is to divide them into three eras based on the motion that most pitchers used in delivering the ball.

The first of these is the underhand era, from 1876 to 1882. In the early days of baseball, pitchers were barely part of the game. Little more than human pitching machines, they tossed the ball softly wherever the batter wanted it, and then they ducked. This began to change when Jim Creighton came along in the early 1860s and subtly violated the rule that forbade pitchers to snap their wrists—what Creighton's contemporaries called "throwing"—as they delivered the ball. Why was the rule not enforced? One reason was natural human competitiveness. Baseball was an increasingly competitive game; because the pitcher was an opponent of the batter, it was only natural that he should try to help his fielders get the batter out. And Albert Spalding recalled that, in those days of scores in the high double figures, enforcing the rule that pitchers had to throw "below the hip, with no bent elbow" began to seem patently unfair. Umpires "permitted the unlawful delivery of the ball rather than stop the game and disappoint the crowd." Henry Chadwick's well-known preference for low-scoring defensive games also may have influenced umpires to tolerate the bending of the pitching rules. The underhand "throw" was legalized in 1872, long after most pitchers had adopted it. As with many of the pitching innovations of the nineteenth century, the official baseball rules lagged years behind what had become common practice.

Pitchers of the underhand era threw a lot like modern fast-pitch softball pitchers, with two exceptions: they had to ease up when there were runners on base, so that their gloveless, padless catchers could stop the ball and prevent the runners from advancing; and they pitched from within a box, marked at the corners by small metal plates, within which they were allowed to run forward as they delivered the ball. They were under the disadvantage of having to throw to a high strike zone (from the waist to the shoulders) or to a low strike zone (from the waist to the knees), according to the batter's wishes. This rule remained in effect until 1887, when the two strike zones were merged into one. From the days of Alexander Cartwright until 1880, the front of the pitcher's box had been 45 feet from home plate. In 1881 the pitching distance was lengthened to 50 feet.

The acceptance of the underhand throw had one revolutionary but entirely unforeseen consequence: the curveball, which cannot be thrown without a sharp snap of the wrist. The wrist snap imparts the tight spin that makes the ball curve. The question of who invented the curveball has been debated by baseball writers and historians for more than a century. The best creation story was told by Arthur "Candy" Cummings. Cummings was a five-foot-nine-inch, 120-pound right-hander who pitched for various Brooklyn teams in the 1860s before going on to have a decent career in the National Association. He then pitched two seasons in the NL, in 1876 and 1877, before retiring in 1878. In an interview given decades later, Cummings tells the following story: "In the summer of 1863 a number of boys and myself were amusing ourselves by throwing clam shells (the hard shell variety) and watching them sail along through the air, turning now to the right, and now to the left. We became interested in the mechanics of it and experimented for an hour or more. All of a sudden it came to me that it would be a good joke on the boys if I could make a baseball curve the same way."[1] Cummings worked and worked until he had learned how to make the ball curve by holding it with a "death grip" and snapping his wrist sharply at the end of his delivery. The new pitch was such a good "joke on the boys" that it carried Cummings through nine professional seasons.

Thanks largely to this interview, Cummings has been generally accepted as the father of the curveball. In 1939 he was elected to the Baseball Hall of Fame for this reason.

There were, however, many other pitchers who claimed to have invented the curve. Alphonse "Phonney" Martin, Tommy Bond, Terry Larkin, Bobby Matthews, and Fred Goldsmith are names that usually come up in curveball creation stories. What all the stories have in common is that the curve was invented within four or five years after Creighton popularized the wrist snap. In 1870 Fred Goldsmith threw the first curve that Henry Chadwick ever saw. Chadwick was so amazed that he staged a public investigation into the new pitch at Brooklyn's Capitoline Grounds. After having set up three poles on a line between the pitcher's box and the plate, he asked Goldsmith, who was standing one side of the first pole, to throw his curve so that it would pass on the far side of the middle pole and then break back, passing to the rear of the third pole. After five or six pitches, Chadwick was satisfied that Goldsmith's curveball was not an optical illusion.

No matter who invented the curveball or when, it is pretty clear from the statistics that few hitters, including major-league players, had faced a really sharp-breaking curve until at least the very late 1870s. It was then that the batting averages of hitters who, like George Wright, could not hit the curve, began to fall off sharply. As late as 1876 Candy Cummings was able to tie NL hitters into knots with his breaking stuff. Pitching for the Hartford Dark Blues in his NL debut against St. Louis, Cummings threw a complete-game shutout. Of the twenty-seven outs made by St. Louis hitters, twenty-four came on pop-ups—twenty-one to the catcher and three to Cummings himself.

Most major-league hitters did not take long, however, to adjust to the underhand curve. After all, the

*Bobby Matthews was one of many who claimed
to have invented the curveball.*

curveball of the underhand era was a far less effective pitch than the modern overhand big bender. It stayed more or less on one plane; and it was slow. Once hitters got the knack of timing it, around the year 1880 or 1881, pitchers began to abandon the curve and return to throwing change-ups—also called dewdrops—and sinkers. Cummings himself went from unhittable to unemployable in less than two NL seasons.

The great pitchers of the underhand era were Al Spalding, Tommy Bond, John Ward, Jim McCormick, Fred Goldsmith, Larry Corcoran, Will White (Deacon White's brother), Old Hoss Radbourn, and Tony Mullane. Most were predominantly fastball and change-up pitchers. Even though men like these were learning how to throw the ball harder and harder, they remained basically everyday players, just like a third baseman or an outfielder. From 1876 to 1882, a major-league team's top pitcher would start between 70 percent and 100 percent of his team's games. Even though nineteenth-century pitchers tried to put the ball in play, and consequently threw many fewer pitches per inning than today's strikeout-oriented pitchers, the innings-pitched totals that they racked up are hard to believe. In 1876 Jim Devlin was the NL leader in innings with 622; the 1882 NL leader Jim McCormick threw 596.

There was no such thing in the underhand era as a bullpen or a pitching rotation in the modern sense. Most teams carried a so-called change pitcher, who played right field. On the rare occasions when the starting pitcher needed a rest, he and the change pitcher would switch positions. Not surprisingly, this system ruined a lot of arms. Corcoran burned out at the age of twenty-four. Ward hurt his arm at twenty-one after pitching 1,182 innings, and winning 87 games, over two seasons. Ward was able to hang on as an extra pitcher and utility man for a few years until his arm healed enough that he could play the infield. He then embarked on a successful second career, playing eleven years at shortstop and second base and batting .278.

The second pitching era is the sidearm era, from 1883 to 1886. Rules allowing pitchers to throw sidearm—that is, with the pitching arm passing as high as the shoulder—were passed by the NL and the AA in 1883 and by the UA in 1884. Pitchers had been using higher and higher arm angles as the underhand era went on, however, and it is likely that many were pitching more or less sidearm well before 1883. Irish-born Tommy Bond was a hard thrower who learned the curve directly from Candy Cummings. He won 40 or more games three years in a row for Boston in the late 1870s, using a controversial high submarine delivery that some felt crossed the line into sidearm. The biggest effect of the new higher angle was to bring back the curveball. Sidearmers put more speed, and therefore more spin, on the ball; and they could make the ball break down instead of just away from the hitter. The best young pitchers to come along in the early 1880s were Tim Keefe and John Clarkson—both of whom learned how to pitch as teenagers from Tommy Bond—Mickey Welch, Guy Hecker, Lady Baldwin, Davy Foutz, Bob Caruthers, and Charlie Sweeney.

Underhand pitching, however, did not immediately become extinct. The best of the underhanders—Old Hoss Radbourn, Pud Galvin, Jim McCormick, and Tony Mullane—were still able to compete and win against the new breed of sidearmers. In fact, what they gave away in speed or breaking stuff, many of the underhanders made up in longevity and durability. Despite having pitched his first game at age twenty-six and having hurt his arm in mid-career, Old Hoss Radbourn managed to earn 308 big-league wins. He pitched 400 innings in a season six times and over 600 innings twice. In one incredible two-year stretch, Radbourn won 109 games with an ERA under 2.00. Tony Mullane, another

Irish-born pitcher, had a thirteen-year career that spanned nearly all of the major pitching changes of the nineteenth century. He won 285 games and completed 469—the ninth-highest career total in history. Mullane pitched right-handed, but he was naturally ambidextrous; on at least one occasion, he switched hands and pitched from the left side to a left-handed hitter.

Pud Galvin was one of the all-time great workhorses. During his fourteen-year career, Galvin pitched more innings than anyone else in history except Cy Young. He is sixth all-time in wins, with 361, and second in complete games, with 639. Like Radbourn, Galvin was on the small side, but he combined a powerful fastball with pinpoint control. During his career he walked only 744 men in almost 6,000 innings. When the last of the underhanders left baseball in the early 1900s, they took the 500-inning season with them. No future generation of pitchers would ever put up numbers like these again.

One of the players most responsible for bringing back the curveball in the early 1880s was not a pitcher but a catcher: Deacon White. White had done a little pitching in the late 1860s when he was a young member of the Cleveland Forest Cities. One day, while experimenting with new deliveries, White hit upon one that allowed him to swing down low and, as he put it, "get my shoulder behind my heave." This was something very similar to the windmill delivery that is used in modern fast-pitch softball. White had some success with the new delivery, but when he and the Forest Cities traveled to Brooklyn to play the famous Mutuals, umpire John Chapman ruled it illegal and threw White out of the game. Sitting in the stands, however, was baseball authority Henry Chadwick, who declared that White's delivery was within the rules.

Deacon White returned to catching soon after this incident, but he developed into a great handler of pitchers and served as a sort of curveball mentor to several generations of players. He taught the curve to dozens of pitchers and improved the technique of dozens of others. White was also a pioneer in the use of the padded glove and the face mask. Thanks to the use of protective equipment, meager as it was by modern standards, White was able to become the first catcher to move up behind the plate full-time and to demonstrate the importance of giving the pitcher a proper target.

In a way, it makes sense that a catcher like White would become a leading pitching innovator and teacher. In spite of the ancient baseball nickname for catcher's equipment—"the tools of ignorance"—the catcher is the most cerebral player on the team. He must set defensive strategy, call the pitches, and handle the pitcher psychologically. Today more catchers become coaches and managers than players from any other position. Back in White's time the relationship between pitcher and catcher was, if anything, even closer than it is in the modern game. There were no pitching coaches in the 1870s and 1880s; by and large, the catcher performed this function. And since catchers of the 1870s and 1880s played without big gloves and significant padding, pitchers and catchers had to work very well together when there were men on base just to enable the catcher to stop the ball and control the running game. It was during this time that the concept of the battery—the idea that the pitcher and catcher had a special relationship and formed a distinct unit within the team—originated. Managers would pair off a pitcher and a catcher because they performed well together. Famous batteries would be advertised to the public as such; sometimes a pitcher and catcher would even be signed, traded, or sold together.

Deacon White was a member of several famous batteries. He caught for early speedball pitcher Al Pratt in his amateur days. He caught for, and taught, great

Curveball pioneer Deacon White

pitchers like Al Spalding in Boston from 1873 to 1875 and in Chicago in 1876. While in Boston, White and Spalding worked a famous nineteenth-century version of the quick pitch: with no one on base, White would sneak up behind the batter, catch the next pitch, and fire it back to Spalding, who would fire it back over the plate before the batter was ready to swing. Deacon White caught for his own brother in 1879, when Will White set an all-time record by completing all 75 of his starts. He caught for Tommy Bond in the first of his three straight 40-win seasons with Boston in 1877. And he guided Pud Galvin early in his career, including catching during Galvin's consecutive 46-win seasons with Buffalo in 1883 and 1884.

A third baseman late in his career, White was also a terrific hitter, batting .303 lifetime. He had his best season in 1877, when he led the NL in batting at .387, in triples with 11, and in RBI's with 49. A member of both nineteenth-century Big Fours—with Boston in 1875 and with Detroit in 1885—White is probably the greatest baseball player not to be elected to the Hall of Fame.

Once pitchers had mastered the curveball and had seen the advantages of pitching from a higher arm angle, the next step was inevitable. In 1884 the NL gave up trying to restrict pitchers' deliveries; the AA followed suit in 1885. The overhand era had arrived. From 1884 on into the 1890s, a new generation of overhand pitchers transformed the game. Young pitchers like Clark Griffith, Ted Breitenstein, Silver King, Kid Nichols, Cy Young, and Amos Rusie along with survivors like Tim Keefe, Bob Caruthers, Tony Mullane, Mickey Welch, and John Clarkson threatened to tip the balance of power drastically in favor of pitching and defense. They overpowered major-league hitters with the unprecedented speed and bewildering variety of new pitches, including the spitball, the screwball, and the scuff ball, that overhand pitching made possible.

The faster, sharper-breaking overhand curveball separated the men from the boys in more ways than one. This is true partly because there have always been great athletes who could run, field, and turn around a 90 mph fastball, but who could not hit a good curveball. There is a classic baseball story about a cocky young prospect who is trying to make a major-league team in spring training. Writing to his mother about his progress, he boasts, "Hitting .300, Ma; these big-league pitchers aren't so tough." His next letter reads: "Hitting .350 now; looks like I'm going to make the team." Finally, in his last letter, he writes, "Coming home tomorrow, Ma; the pitchers started throwing curveballs today."

Just as importantly, the overhand curveball introduced a new element of fear into the game. From 1884 until today right-handed hitters facing right-handed pitchers have had to deal, virtually on a daily basis, with that terrible moment of uncertainty when they are not sure whether the pitch coming at them is an errant high fastball rushing toward the middle of their skull or a harmless curveball about to break away and across the plate. The consequences of guessing wrong can be very serious or even fatal. Because most pitchers are, of course, right-handed, left-handed hitters have the advantage of experiencing fewer such moments. When Al Spalding made his second baseball tour abroad in 1888 and 1889, even the baseball-ignorant English noticed the difference. One English reporter who had witnessed Spalding and Wright's first tour in 1874 wrote, "It is certain that the striker [hitter] was not so terribly handicapped as now. The game, consequently, as played fifteen years ago, was far more lively and interesting to Englishmen than it is in its present perfection. The pitcher seems to have it all his own way now."[2]

Baseball rule makers fought a series of holding actions against the effects of overhand pitching, but within a year or two the pitchers always regained their dominance over the hitters. In 1887 the pitcher was forced to keep his back foot on the back line of the pitcher's box; this effectively lengthened the pitching distance by two feet. Also in that year the number of strikes required for a strikeout was raised to four. In the NL the combined result of these measures was to raise the league ERA from 3.31 to 4.05. Only a year later, after pitchers had adjusted to the new delivery and the strikeout rule had been changed back to three strikes, the league ERA dropped back to 2.83. In 1889, to help the hitters, the number of balls required for a walk was reduced to four, and the NL ERA jumped back up to 4.02. Still, the pitchers recovered quickly. The NL ERA fell to 3.60 in 1890, 3.34 in 1891, and 3.28 in 1892.

Leading the pitching counterattack of the early 1890s were Amos Rusie and Denton True "Cy" Young. Called Cy because his fastball moved like a cyclone, Young was as consistent and durable as any pitcher who has ever lived. He began to win from the moment he put on a major-league uniform. Fresh from his Ohio farm in 1890, Young celebrated his major-league debut with Cleveland by defeating the Chicago White Stockings 8–1 and striking out the great Cap Anson twice. An impressed Anson tried unsuccessfully to buy the rookie pitcher on the spot for $1,000.

With a sharp curve, a hard fastball, and later on, a spitter, Cy Young pitched for twenty-two seasons and won 511 games, the highest total in major-league history. This is the record that is most often brought up when fans discuss the baseball records that are least likely ever to be broken. To put Young's achievement in perspective, all-time great Walter Johnson pitched for twenty-one years and fell 95 wins short. Young, who hated to practice and hated to throw to first, believing that there were only so many throws in a man's arm, completed an amazing 751 out of 815 lifetime starts and pitched an all-time record 7,356 innings. While he never threw 500 innings in a season like an Old Hoss Radbourn or Jim McCormick, Young pitched longer and better than the underhand workhorses of the 1880s. For the decade of the 1890s Young's average seasonal record was 27-15 with a 3.05 ERA; the following decade, he averaged 27-15, but with an ERA of 2.12. He recorded ERAs below 2.00 in six different seasons and never had an ERA over 4.00. An overweight but still effective Young retired in 1912 at the age of forty-four, saying his arm felt fine but that he could no longer field his position.

Indiana-born Amos Rusie, known as the Hoosier Thunderbolt, was the Nolan Ryan of the 1890s. At six-one, 220 pounds, he threw harder than any of his contemporaries and mixed in a curve that broke, it was said, "straight down, like a rock." He struck out hitters at an unheard-of rate, whiffing three hundred men three times, he led the NL in strikeouts every year from 1890 to 1895, but he was wild. Rusie averaged more than 170 walks per season and led the NL in walks five times.

What was it like to face pitchers like Amos Rusie or Cy Young from 55 feet 6 inches away? The NL gave its answer in 1893 when it replaced the pitcher's box with the pitching rubber and moved the pitcher back 5 feet to 60 feet 6 inches from home plate—the present distance. From 1893 until today there have been no major changes in the rules governing pitching distance and pitchers' deliveries. Remarkably, the strain of having to throw the ball five more feet had little short-term effect on Young and even less on Rusie: his ERA went from 2.88 to 3.23, and he completed 50 out of 52 starts. Overall, however, the new pitching distance gave the edge back to the hitters in a big way. The NL ERA soared to 4.66; Billy Hamilton of the Philadelphia Athletics hit .380; and two teams batted .300. The following year the effects of the new pitching distance were still being felt. In 1894 the NL ERA rose to an ugly 5.32

and the entire league batted .309. Boston's Hugh Duffy hit .438, the highest single-season batting average of all time.

Thanks to 1893, major-league-hitters put up numbers in the 1890s that had not been seen since the 1870s. Later in the decade, however, pitchers began to turn back the tide. ERAs fell back into the middle and low 4.00s and a few more batters hit .400, but no one challenged Duffy's record. Not until the early 1900s, after a long, hard climb—and with a little help from the rule makers—would major-league pitchers fully recover from 1893 and reassert their control over the game in what was aptly referred to as the Dead Ball era.

CHAPTER SEVEN

They Never Had It Made: Minor-League Expansion and the First Integration of Baseball

In baseball's early amateur days the game was strictly racially segregated; a so-called color line divided white baseball from African-American baseball. This was nothing unusual. Most baseball clubs and town ball clubs of the 1840s and 1850s were based in northern cities like Boston, New York, and Philadelphia, where racial segregation was the rule in churches, restaurants, streetcars, and nearly all other public and social institutions. Baseball's first national organization, the NABBP, was firmly committed to the color line and passed a rule forbidding clubs "composed of colored men, or any white clubs having colored members" to join. In those days baseball clubs were largely middle-class institutions that were very concerned with respectability. For most middle-class northerners, it was part of being respectable to exclude African-Americans, Catholics, Jews, and members of other minority groups.

With the collapse of the NABBP and the birth of baseball's first professional leagues in the 1870s and 1880s, however, African-American ballplayers began here and there to cross the color line and play with white clubs. Other than a few short-lived attempts, there were no professional leagues on the African-American side of the color line; the only professional opportunity for a baseball player on the African-American side of the color line was to join an independent, or barnstorming, club. These clubs would tour the country playing local teams for a share of the gate.

Why were African-Americans suddenly allowed to cross the baseball color line? Part of the reason was the explosive proliferation of new clubs and new minor leagues; many of these new leagues were in the Midwest and West, where racial segregation was less ingrained than in the Northeast. Another factor was professionalism itself: with teams competing to make money and to win, there was more pressure to sign players based on skill rather than on skin color. Finally, in the aftermath of the Civil War and the Reconstruction period, America as a whole entered a period of liberalization in racial attitudes and relations. Not until the middle to late 1890s would strict segregationism become the universal rule in American society.

Still, the door did not open wide. The number of African-American ballplayers allowed to cross the color line never approached the number who were good enough to compete in white baseball. Acceptance of African-Americans in baseball was grudging and, usually, temporary. African-American ballplayers enjoyed little job security; white teams hired them only when— and for as long as—they had no alternative.

This tentative integration of baseball could not have happened without the success of professionalism and the development of the major and minor leagues. The 1870s, 1880s, and 1890s saw the creation of dozens of new leagues with hundreds of new teams and thousands of new playing jobs that had to be filled. The vast majority of these jobs were in the minor leagues. The first two major leagues, like the NABBP, strictly observed the tradition of the baseball color line. Neither the NA nor the NL admitted a single African-American club or African-American player in the nineteenth century. (One possible exception was Esteban Bellan, who played fifty-nine NA games for the Troy Haymakers and the New York Mutuals before returning home to play baseball in his native Cuba.) As had been the case with the first amateur baseball clubs, there was no written rule excluding African-Americans, only what was known as the gentleman's agreement. Outside of the stuffy, class-conscious NA and NL, however, the rationale for the color line was eroding quickly during this period.

In 1877 the first three minor leagues were formed, and two of them joined the NL in signing the National Agreement. This was the beginning of the major-league–minor-league alliance that later came to be called organized baseball. It was followed by an explosion of new professional leagues and clubs. While many of these did not last long and there was much coming and going of leagues, clubs, and players, on the whole the 1880s was a decade of across-the-board expansion for professional baseball. The major leagues expanded from eight teams to fourteen with the advent of the AA in 1882; this figure increased to sixteen in 1883 and thirty-four in 1884, the year of the UA and Monopoly War II. The major leagues were eventually reduced to a single twelve-team league, but the minors continued to grow. From 1883 to 1890, the number of minor leagues that affiliated themselves with major-league baseball increased to seventeen. But this number does not include the dozens of smaller or independent minor leagues that came and went during this time.

These changes weakened the color line. With no link to the cultural traditions of the NABBP, many new minor-league clubs saw no reason not to sign promising African-Americans. Dozens of them signed players from the crack African-American independent teams that had sprung up on the model of the famous Cuban Giants. The Cuban Giants were neither Cuban nor giants; their name came from the fact that "Cuban" was a euphemism of the time for "dark-skinned" and the fact that the New York Giants of Jim Mutrie, Roger Connor, John Ward, Buck Ewing, and Tim Keefe were by far the most popular major-league club on the East Coast. Originally a team made up of employees of the Argyle Hotel, a fashionable beach resort in Babylon, Long Island, the Cuban Giants went independent and became the first great African-American professional club.

Integration in baseball reached the point that in 1887, when several African-American clubs in the North joined forces to form an African-American professional league, the League of Colored Baseball Clubs (LCBC), they signed onto the National Agreement as an official minor league. Their purpose was to protect their rosters from being raided by white minor-league clubs. This was a very real concern, although, as it turned out, the LCBC lasted less than a year. By the end of the 1890s at least fifty-five African-Americans would play on white teams in organized baseball.

Most of those fifty-five men played in the low minor leagues; only a handful of the best and most determined were able to work their way up to the high minors. In 1884, the year of thirty-four major-league teams and a great drought of baseball talent, a pair of African-American brothers named Fleet and Welday Walker did the unthinkable: they played in the major leagues. They reached the majors partly by accident when their team, Toledo, Ohio, of the Northwestern League, was absorbed by the American Association as part of its strategy to deny markets to the rival Union Association.

The very first African-American to enter white baseball never played in the major leagues, but not for lack of ability—he was a better player than either of the Walker brothers. His name was John Fowler. He was known as Bud because of his habit of calling strangers by that name. Bud Fowler was born in 1858, ironically enough, in Cooperstown, New York. After cutting his baseball teeth with the African-American Mutuals of Washington, D.C., Fowler played on his first white team in 1872 in New Castle, Pennsylvania. His career in organized baseball ended in 1895 with a brief appearance in the Michigan State League twenty-three years later. In between, he played with twenty teams in thirteen leagues, most of them in the West and Midwest. Bouncing back and forth between the minor leagues and the world of African-American baseball, he never played more than one season with the same white team. Because of his race, Fowler was never welcome for very long.

Bud Fowler's career typified the experience of dozens of other African-Americans who would cross the color line after him. Fowler never knew what to expect from white fans, teammates, or the press. In most communities where he played, he was the first African-American anyone had ever seen playing on a white club. Reaction to him ranged from respect and affection to blind hatred. Newspaper stories about Fowler are full of strange racial jokes that say a lot about the discomfort many whites felt when faced with integration. The *Sporting Life* wrote with tongue in cheek that "some say that Fowler is a colored man, but we account for his dark complexion by the fact that . . . in chasing balls [he] has become tanned from constant and careless exposure to the sun."

In 1887, while playing with Binghamton, New York, of the International League, Fowler encountered the worst racial hostility of his career. Competitively, the

International League of the 1880s was at least the equivalent of a Triple-A league today; some IL teams may actually have been better than some major-league outfits. Fowler was not the only African-American player in the IL; Frank Grant was playing for Buffalo, and Fleet Walker and George Stovey were with Newark. But there was a lot of opposition around the league to the hiring of African-Americans. One IL veteran anonymously told the *Sporting News* in 1889: "Fowler used to play second base with the lower part of his legs encased in wooden guards. He knew that about every player that came down to second base on a steal had it in for him and would, if possible, throw the spikes into him. He was a good player, but left the base every time there was a close play in order to get away from the spikes."[1]

Fowler was released from the team in mid-July. He was batting .350.

Bud Fowler learned that an African-American had to be much better than a white player even to be considered for a job. As a result, most of the African-Americans who played in the high minors in the nineteenth century were stars; mediocre white players were never in short supply. And in spite of the many obstacles put in his way, Fowler produced on the baseball field. He hit .320 in the Northwestern League, .309 in the Western League, .343 in the New Mexico League, and .331 in the Michigan State League. In the end, however, he was worn down and driven back into the world of African-American baseball for good. Talking with a reporter shortly after he retired from baseball, he said, "My skin is against me. If I had been not quite so black, I might have caught on as a Spaniard or something of that kind. The race prejudice is so strong that my black skin barred me."

Fowler was being modest. Even the white sporting press recognized that Fowler had enough ability not only to catch on, but to become a major-league star. In 1885, for example, the *Sporting Life* rated Fowler as "one of the best general players in the country" and stated that "if he had a white face, he would be playing with the best of them." Indeed, if Fowler had been white, a Cap Anson or a Frank Bancroft would undoubtedly have plucked him from the dusty diamonds of Keokuk, Topeka, or Santa Fe and given him a job where he belonged—in the major leagues.

Bud Fowler devoted much of the rest of his life to developing and managing independent African-American teams. He founded a number of famous barnstorming clubs, including the Page Fence Giants and the All-American Black Tourists. In 1904 he failed in an attempt to organize an African-American league.

Catcher Moses Fleetwood "Fleet" Walker crossed the color line in 1883. Walker was a rarity in nineteenth-century baseball—and not just because he was African-American. In a world where a player who went to church, studied law, or chose not to drink and gamble stood out so much that he was labeled with a derisive nickname like Deacon, Orator, or Parson, Walker was one of the rare college men. The son of a minister from Steubenville, Ohio, Walker attended Oberlin College, a liberal arts school where he studied Latin, Greek, German, engineering, and rhetoric. In 1882 he transferred to the University of Michigan, where he started at catcher on the varsity baseball team and caught the attention of professional baseball men. Photographs from his Oberlin days show a tall, handsome man with a refined, gentlemanly demeanor.

Walker was certainly a gentleman, but he was also as tough as nails—to play catcher in the 1880s, he had to be. He went professional in 1883 with Toledo of the minor Northwestern League. Toledo won the pennant that year with Walker starting at catcher. The following year the Toledo franchise joined the American Association and brought along its top players. Fleet Walker was one of them.

Walker played well in his one major-league season, and he was tremendously popular among the fans of Toledo. Around the rest of the league, however, reaction to him was, as it had been with Bud Fowler, mixed. In Louisville, racist fans booed and heckled him. In more liberal cities Walker and Toledo's starting pitcher, Tony Mullane, were a surefire gate attraction. Aside from the ethnic curiosity of a battery made up of an African-American and an Irishman, they were a winning combination on the field. Mullane had one of his finest seasons with Fleet Walker catching him. He pitched in 68 games, completed 65 and won 37, all second only to league-leader Guy Hecker, and he led the AA in shutouts with 8. Remembering the 1884 season years later, Mullane conceded that Walker was "the best catcher I ever worked with." But Fleet Walker was faced with a hardship that few other AA catchers had to deal with. Mullane went on to say in the same interview, "I disliked a Negro and whenever I pitched to him I used to pitch anything I wanted without looking at his signals."

Whether being constantly crossed up by Mullane had anything to do with it or not, Walker hurt his ribs late in the 1884 season and was released. In 1885 he signed with Cleveland of the minor Western League, joining his brother Welday, who had filled in for a few games in the outfield with Toledo in 1884. Neither the Walkers nor any other African-American would appear again in the major leagues for sixty-two years. Fleet Walker went on to star in the International League with Syracuse, New York, and Newark, New Jersey. At Newark he and pitcher George Stovey formed organized baseball's first ever all-African-American battery. Walker retired at age thirty-three on a high note after helping Syracuse win the 1889 IL pennant.

Like Bud Fowler, Fleet Walker was a talented man who might have contributed much more to baseball, both during and after his career, if it had not been for the color line. After leaving the game Walker returned to Steubenville where he became a successful business-man and a leader of the African-American community. In spite of his success, Walker's experiences in and out of baseball left him profoundly pessimistic about the future of African-Americans in this country. In a 1908 book called *Our Home Colony*, he urged African-Americans to emigrate to Africa.

The third great African-American star to play in the minor leagues in the 1880s was second baseman Frank Grant. Many argue that Grant, not Bud Fowler, was the greatest African-American baseball player of the nineteenth century. Grant was the only African-American of his time to play three consecutive seasons with the same white club—Buffalo in the International League.

Grant batted .313 or higher in every one of his six seasons in organized baseball. Although he was below average in size, he hit for power and was an excellent base runner. He regularly had stolen base totals in double digits and was famous for his ability to steal home. African-American baseball player, entrepreneur, and historian Sol White wrote that Grant's play was "a revelation to his fellow teammates, as well as the spectators. In hitting he ranked with the best and his fielding bordered on the impossible." One of the greatest tributes from the white press to a nineteenth-century African-American player came when the *Sporting Life* named Frank Grant as the greatest player ever to have played in Buffalo. This put him at the top of a list that included four future Hall of Famers: Pud Galvin, Dan Brouthers, Orator O'Rourke, and Old Hoss Radbourn.

Grant was worshiped by the Buffalo fans. However, as with Walker and Fowler before him, he was not so popular among his fellow players. In 1886 and 1888 his own teammates refused to pose with him for the team picture. They made it clear that the reason was nothing personal—it was just the color of his skin.

After leaving organized baseball, Frank Grant played with the Cuban Giants and the New York Gorhams in the 1890s. In the early 1900s Grant played with the Philadelphia Giants, an independent team that dominated African-American baseball for a decade. He retired in 1903 and spent the rest of his life working as a waiter in a New York City restaurant.

Fowler, Walker, and Grant were able to cross the color line and play in white baseball for two main reasons. One was a temporary thaw in American race relations. The other was simple economic necessity: African-American players were needed to fill the greatly increasing number of professional baseball jobs in the 1880s. The number of African-American jobs in organized baseball had expanded with the economy. It contracted with the economy, too, however. When America suffered a depression in 1891 and 1892, followed by a long period of sluggish economic growth, two things happened: the number of baseball leagues and teams shrank drastically, and the number of African-Americans in white baseball dropped to zero. Either way, what Fowler and the others accomplished had been unthinkable before the 1870s and would become unthinkable again soon after 1887.

Sometime around the year 1887 organized baseball seems to have decided that integration had to go. There was even a backlash in parts of the normally liberal press, which felt threatened by the increasing African-American presence in the IL, baseball's top minor league. "How far will this mania for engaging colored players go?" sneered the *Sporting Life*, "At the present rate of progress the International League may ere many moons change its name to the 'Colored League.'" At a secret meeting in July of 1887 the IL board of directors voted to ban the hiring of any more African-Americans.

One particular racial incident attracted national attention and came to symbolize the spirit of 1887. It occurred on a July afternoon in Newark, New Jersey. A crowd of three thousand fans had turned out for an exhibition game between the Newark Little Giants, and Cap Anson's Chicago White Stockings. There were two reasons for the big crowd that day. One was the chance to see the great Anson and his lineup of NL stars. The other drawing card was Newark's popular African-American battery of George Stovey and Fleet Walker. The fans were eager to see how Stovey, the IL's best pitcher that year—he went on to win thirty-four games, still an IL record—would do against Anson, the NL's best hitter. Unfortunately, the dream match-up was not to be. Before the game, Anson told Newark that he would pull his team from the field unless they replaced the African-Americans with white players. Facing three thousand ticket refunds, Newark gave in. Stovey and Walker were benched. The reason soon leaked out. A Toronto newspaper reported that "[Newark manager Charlie] Hackett intended putting Stovey in the box against the Chicagos, but Anson objected to his playing on account of his color."

As the Newark incident shows, the year 1887 was a turning point for race relations and baseball. Within a few years after Anson intimidated Newark into benching Walker and Stovey, the IL rid itself of its remaining African-American players. Other minor leagues followed the IL's lead and soon organized baseball was as lily-white as it had been in the days of the Knickerbockers, Eagles, and Empires. The last appearances by African-Americans in the white minors occurred far outside the baseball mainstream, in small-time leagues in Kansas and Michigan. In the middle 1890s some of

Bud Fowler's Page Fence Giants, who were based in Adrian, Michigan, played briefly for Adrian's entry in the Michigan State League. Adrian was in a pennant race and borrowed Bud Fowler and a few of his players for the last few weeks of the season. Ironically Adrian, Michigan, is the town that gave Adrian "Cap" Anson his first name.

The very last African-American to appear in nineteenth-century organized baseball was Bert Jones. Nicknamed the "Yellow Kid" after the first popular newspaper comic-strip character, Jones was a fire-balling lefthander who pitched for Atchison in the Kansas State League in 1897 and 1898. From Bert Jones until Jackie Robinson, Jim Crow reigned supreme over the national game.

Because of the national publicity surrounding the 1887 Newark incident, Cap Anson has gone down in baseball history as the main reason for this. As influential as Anson may have been in the 1880s, however, to imagine that he had the power to single-handedly banish African-Americans from every league in every city in North America is patently ridiculous. In fact, long before the Newark incident, the White Stockings had objected to playing against teams with African-American players. In 1884 Albert Spalding's secretary wrote on behalf of his boss to the Toledo AA club about an upcoming exhibition game between the two teams. He reminded Toledo of its earlier promise to Spalding not to allow that "colored man"—Fleet Walker—to take the field. Brown claimed that "the management of the Chicago club have no personal feeling about the matter," but that "the players do most decisively object."

Like their counterparts from the 1930s and 1940s, nineteenth-century team owners and league officials often used the prejudices of players like Anson to justify racist policies, but there is good reason to suspect that this was nothing but an excuse. The 1880s and 1890s, after all, were a historic low point in player salaries, rights, and influence over how the game was run. The owners did not consider the feelings of Anson or any other player when, in 1887, they made the hated reserve clause part of every contract—or when they instituted a salary cap two years later. Clearly, responsibility for the reintroduction of the baseball color line must lie with the men who made the rest of the decisions for the baseball monopoly—the owners.

As they would convincingly demonstrate by their high-handed, dictatorial behavior during the Players League affair of 1889 and 1890, Albert Spalding and his fellow baseball owners did not care one bit what the players thought about anything else; why would they have cared how they felt about playing with African-Americans?

"*I*s the Base-Ball Player a Chattel?": John Montgomery Ward and the Players League Revolt

It was a bad idea to underestimate John Montgomery Ward. One of the NL's top pitchers from the moment he signed with Providence in 1878, Ward came down with a sore arm in 1882. Even after he'd spent two years on part-time duty, his arm still had not bounced back; Ward was through as a major-league pitcher. Only twenty-four years old, he had a record of 161-101 and an ERA of 2.10—the fourth-best career ERA of all time.

But Ward did not quit. He signed with the New York Giants as a utility man and worked hard to improve his hitting and fielding. In 1885 he won the Giants' starting shortstop job and hit .226. He hit .273 in 1886 and .338 the year after that. If you made a list of all the baseball skills that can be acquired through intelligence, practice, and hard work, you would have a pretty good description of the kind of ballplayer John Ward had become by the late 1880s. He was not fast, but on technique and pure smarts he stole 111 bases in one season. He drew walks and got on base. In 1888, at the age of twenty-eight, he even experimented with switch-hitting.

Sheet music for "The Home Run Polka." Note the artist's apparent confusion over whether the Nationals played baseball, townball, or cricket.

The Giants won the NL pennant in 1888 and 1889; Ward was a star on a team of stars, among them Roger Connor, Hardie Richardson, Mike Tiernan, Orator O'Rourke, Buck Ewing, Mickey Welch, and Tim Keefe. Through Keefe, Ward met Helen Dauvray, a beautiful stage actress; they fell in love and married in 1887. Dauvray introduced Ward to New York nightlife, and the handsome couple became a hit in downtown society. In 1888 the popular Ward published *Ward's BaseBall Book*, a baseball instructional. Somehow he also found the time to earn degrees in law and political science from Columbia University.

Because of his legal training Ward was asked by his fellow players to head up baseball's first labor organization, the National Brotherhood of Professional Baseball Players. At the time the Brotherhood, as it was known, could hardly have been called a union; it had been formed in the summer of 1885 for the benign purpose of raising a fund to help ballplayers with medical bills and emergency expenses. In the beginning, tearing down the major-league monopoly and eliminating the reserve clause were the furthest things from Ward's mind. In fact, when asked by a reporter about the reserve clause, Ward gave a reply that might have come from the mouth of Albert Spalding:

> *In order to get men to invest capital in Base Ball, it is necessary to have a reserve rule. Some say that this could be modified, but I am not of that opinion. How could it be modified? Say, for instance, that we began this season by reserving men for only two, three, four or even five years. At the expiration of that period players would be free to go where they pleased, and the capitalists who invested, say, $75,000 or $100,000, would have nothing but ground and grandstand . . . The reserve rule on the whole is a bad one, but it cannot be rectified save by injuring the interests of the men who invest their money, and that is not the object of the Brotherhood.*[1]

Ward's Brotherhood, however, was soon radicalized by a series of events that resembled the labor-management conflicts of the 1980s and 1990s. The first of these came in the late fall of 1885, when the major-league owners announced that they would impose a salary cap of $2,000 per year per player. This infuriated the players because salaries had risen to many times that amount during the interleague bidding wars of 1882, 1883, and 1884. A crisis was averted, however, by the owners' own selfishness; most owners cheated on the new system by paying players off the books any part of their salary that exceeded the $2,000 limit.

The next few years were a time of peaceful coexistence between the NL and the AA. Owner profits grew, attendance figures soared, and the World Series was invented. The players, however, felt increasingly left out of all this prosperity. The salary cap may have fizzled, but the reserve clause and the blacklisting rule still kept their pay artificially low. Owners had unlimited power to fine or suspend players, and they repeatedly abused this power. A wronged player had no recourse except to appeal to a six-man panel chosen by the clubs. A series of blockbuster player sales reminded the players that they earned only a fraction of what they were worth on the open market. In 1885 Buffalo's Big Four—Rowe, Richardson, Brouthers, and White—were sold to Detroit for $7,000. In 1886 Chicago sold King Kelly to Boston for a record $10,000; a year after that, Chicago sold John Clarkson to Boston for the same amount. None of the players in these deals received a penny of the purchase price; some of them did not even get a raise from their new team.

The straw that broke the camel's back came in 1888 when the Detroit franchise put its entire roster on the block in what amounted to a going-out-of-business sale. Two former members of the Big Four, Deacon White and Jack Rowe, went to Pittsburgh for $7,000. This time, however, White had had enough of being sold like a piece of meat. He refused to report to

Pittsburgh; instead, he and Rowe bought the minor-league team in White's hometown of Buffalo and put themselves on the Buffalo roster. When Pittsburgh went to court to try to stop White and Rowe from playing for Buffalo, saying that they were on Pittsburgh's reserve list and therefore ineligible to play for themselves, players and fans across the country were outraged. In the end, with the help of Ward, a compromise was reached. White and Rowe reported to Pittsburgh at generous salaries of $5,000 a year; Pittsburgh kicked in signing bonuses of $1,250 each. "We are satisfied with the money," the plainspoken White told a Buffalo news-paper, "but we ain't worth it. Rowe's arm is gone and my fielding ain't so good, though I can still hit some. But I will say this. No man is going to sell my carcass unless I get half."

At first, Ward and the Brotherhood focused on try-ing to right little wrongs, like the many cases of petty mistreatment and shortchanging of players by their clubs. Ward embarrassed the owners into making good on a $100 bonus check that Washington owner John Gaffney had given outfielder Cliff Carroll as an induce-ment to sign a contract and had then stopped payment on. This kind of abuse was not at all uncommon. Boston owner Arthur Soden fined and suspended slug-ger Charley Jones without pay when Jones demanded almost $400 in salary that Soden owed him. Jones appealed to the NL central office, but the league refused to intervene. He went to court and won, but still the league refused to act. In the end, Jones spent two long years on Boston's blacklist, supported by the pro-ceeds of benefit games played by friends and team-mates, before the AA came along in 1882 and gave him a job. Fed up with being fined unfairly by their owner, the entire Louisville team went on strike for two days.

Before long, Ward recognized that the real problem was the reserve clause. In an article entitled "Is the

Base-Ball Player a Chattel?", which appeared in the prestigious *Lippincott's Magazine*, Ward compared the reserve system to slavery. "Like a fugitive slave law," he argued, "the reserve rule denies [the player] a harbor or a livelihood, and carries him back, bound and shackled, to the club from which he attempted to escape." Only three decades after the end of the Civil War, these were fighting words. Yet Ward moved cautiously. He had several meetings with major-league officials, at which the concerns of players and owners were discussed in a friendly way. As Ward was soon to learn, however, the owners had no real intention of compromising; they were stringing him along until they could implement their latest idea—a rigid salary classification system that would fix player salaries according to where they ranked in performance on a scale of A through E. An A player would make $2,500 a year, a B player $2,250, and so on down to $1,500 for an E player. A ridiculous feature of the plan was that the rankings would be determined by the league presidents. For the time being, the owners kept the classification scheme a secret.

In 1888 Ward and the Brotherhood agreed to let the owners spell out the reserve clause in the standard player contract; previously the owners had claimed the clause as an implicit right. In return, the owners agreed to consider lifting the salary cap and promised not to cut the salary of any player whose contract was renewed for 1889. Trusting the owners' word, Ward agreed to join Spalding's around-the-world baseball tour of 1888–1889. This off-season tour consisted of a series of games played by the Chicago White Stockings against a so-called All-America team made up of major-league players from other teams, including John Ward, pitcher Ned "Cannonball" Crane, and outfielder Ned Hanlon. Accompanying the ballplayers was a motley crew that included Al Spalding, Spalding's mother, Cap

Anson's father, several reporters, and the Chicago team mascot, an African-American man named Clarence Duval. It was common for teams of the late nineteenth century to hire African-American mascots who would clown around in colorful costumes during games; baseball superstition held that kissing or rubbing the head of an African-American would bring good luck. The tour stopped in Hawaii—missing connections with the seventy-eight-year-old Alexander Cartwright by a few hours—and put on baseball exhibitions before crowds of puzzled onlookers in Australia, Ceylon (now Sri Lanka), and Egypt, before reaching continental Europe and then their final destination, England.

When the ship carrying Spalding's baseball tourists arrived in New York City on the morning of April 6, 1889, George Gore and a small group of major-league players were standing on the dock; they had been waiting all night. Gore informed Ward that while he was away, the owners had implemented their salary classification plan, in effect breaking their word not to renew player contracts at lower salaries. Livid, Ward spent the next several days trying to meet with Spalding to discuss the matter. "There is nothing to discuss," Spalding replied.

It was too late to fight the salary classification system for 1889, but Ward and the players soon came up with a plan of their own. At a Brotherhood meeting on Bastille Day, July 14, 1889, Ward stated publicly that the players were seeking backing for a new league. Four months later Ward fired the opening shot in Monopoly War III by unveiling a new cooperative baseball organization called the Players National League, or the PL. The league would not use the reserve clause; all players would be given three-year contracts and the right to work out transfers to other clubs for themselves. Gate receipts were to be split fifty-fifty among all the clubs. After the first $10,000, investors were also to share club profits fifty-fifty with the players. The league would be overseen by a board of directors composed of both players and investors.

The Brotherhood issued a manifesto in which it condemned the major-league owners for their greedy, high-handed behavior. It read, in part:

> There was a time when [major-league baseball] stood for integrity and fair dealing. Today it stands for dollars and cents. Once it looked to the elevation of the game and an honest exhibition of the sport; today its eyes are upon the turnstile. Men have come into the business for no other motive than to exploit it for every dollar in sight. . . The reserve rule and the provisions of the National Agreement gave the managers unlimited power, and they have not hesitated to use this in the most arbitrary and mercenary way. Players have been bought, sold and exchanged as though they were sheep instead of American citizens.[2]

The PL had attracted an impressive list of well-heeled investors, including trolley-car operator Albert Johnson of Cincinnati, stockbroker Edward Talcott of New York, real estate dealer Wendell Goodwin of Brooklyn, and contractor John Addison of Chicago. Ward's strategy was to compete directly with the NL and AA for the largest markets. When the eight-team PL opened for business in 1890, it would field franchises in New York, Boston, Chicago, Philadelphia, Brooklyn, Cleveland, Pittsburgh, and Buffalo.

Ward's plan for a new league was not as unrealistic as it might sound to a modern baseball fan. In the days before national television contracts, cable deals and billion-dollar stadiums, start-up costs for a baseball league or a baseball club were very low. And, as the players were well aware, only eight years earlier the AA had taken on and defeated the NL monopoly. The Brotherhood had acted out of idealism, and it followed through on its ideals. When, in the end, the PL failed, it was not the players who had given in but the nervous bankers and businessmen who had backed them. Ward's Players League could have—and probably should have—succeeded; when the final attendance figures for the 1890 season were all in, the PL had outdrawn the NL and AA by a wide margin. Even Al Spalding admitted later that both the AA and NL had been on the financial ropes. In Monopoly War III the winning side had surrendered.

By the spring of 1890, despite the best efforts of Spalding and fellow owner John Brush to persuade or intimidate players into staying, most major-league players had flocked to the PL. This included nearly every well-known star. Charles Comiskey, Orator O'Rourke, Roger Connor, Pete Browning, Buck Ewing, Tip O'Neill, Harry Stovey, Old Hoss Radbourn, Pud Galvin, and Hugh Duffy were just a few of the big names to defect. Virtually the only major star to remain in the NL was Chicago's Cap Anson, who was motivated by loyalty either to Spalding or to his own bank account. Anson owned stock in the White Stockings and may well have considered himself a part of management.

The owners tried bribery, but to little avail. In his 1911 memoir Spalding tells the story of how he offered the perpetually broke King Kelly money to desert the PL. To bring a superstar like Kelly back into the fold, Spalding knew, would be a body blow to Brotherhood morale. Meeting with Kelly at a hotel, Spalding placed a check for $10,000, made out to Kelly, on a table; he also handed him a three-year contract and told him to fill in the salary figures himself. "What does this mean?" Kelly asked with a stricken look. "Does it mean that I'm going to join the league? Quit the Brotherhood? Go back on the boys?" After Spalding told him that that was exactly what it meant, Kelly went out for a long walk. Returning an hour and a half later, he told Spalding that his answer was no. "What? You don't want the $10,000?" Spalding asked in disbelief. "Aw, I want the ten thousand bad enough," Kelly said, "but I've thought the matter over, and I can't go back on the boys." Kelly then borrowed $500 from Spalding and left.

The owners' next move was to go to court to seek injunctions preventing individual reserved players from playing for the PL. To the owners' surprise, however, the courts ruled consistently in the players' favor. A New York judge released John Ward from any obligation to the Giants, ruling that the Giants were not damaged because they had replaced Ward with a player of equal value—Jack Glasscock, one of the few Brotherhood members who had gone back to the NL—and that the reserve clause was illegal. In the case of Buck Ewing, another New York judge rejected the owners' interpretation of the reserve clause, calling it "merely a contract to make a contract if the parties can agree." These rulings sent the owners into a state of shock. Boston's Arthur Soden explained to the press that the judges' problem was that they just did not understand baseball.

Facing their worst nightmare—free-market competition—Spalding and his fellow magnates declared all-out war. In cities where there was both a PL and an NL franchise, the NL scheduled its games at the same time as the PL contests. This was virtual business suicide, because in the early part of the 1890 season, the PL was heavily outdrawing the NL. In the end, however, this tactic weakened both leagues. A public relations war broke out over attendance figures as both sides lied through their teeth in order to demoralize the opposition. Charges flew in the press; the players were accused of being terrorists and anarchists. After the *Sporting News*, the country's leading baseball weekly, endorsed the PL, Spalding pulled all Spalding Sporting Goods Company advertising out of the newspaper and started up a new pro-NL weekly called the *Sporting Times*. More and more baseball fans became disillusioned by all the name-calling and backbiting. Henry Chadwick wrote that "the simple fact is that the interest in the championship games is gone. None are asking, 'Who leads in the pennant race?'"

By late summer of 1890 it was clear that Spalding had lost the battle for the hearts and minds of the fans; it was equally clear that he had not put a dent in the players' loyalty to the Brotherhood. But Spalding had succeeded in one all-important area: he had spooked many of the wealthy capitalists who were backing the PL. Thanks in part to Spalding's scorched-earth policies, the three major leagues had lost an estimated one million dollars. The NL was stronger than the AA, but that was not saying much; NL franchises in Cincinnati and Pittsburgh were bankrupt, and the New York Giants had been saved from a similar fate only by the infusion of $80,000 from Spalding and three other NL owners.

Spalding's strategy was to hide the losses suffered by his side and exaggerate the losses of the PL clubs. He hoped to bluff the PL into thinking that the NL could afford to hold out indefinitely. Spalding's bluff worked. In July 1890 a group of major PL investors had a failure of nerve; meeting secretly with Spalding, they sold out the Brotherhood and agreed to a merger of the PL and NL franchises in Chicago, Pittsburgh, and New York. Former PL backers, including Talcott and Addison, were allowed to buy into the NL clubs in their home cities. Unable to continue without the key Chicago and New York franchises, the PL immediately folded. Monopoly War III was over.

The NL and AA reinstituted the reserve clause and the salary classification system for 1891 and announced that all players would become the property of the clubs that had previously reserved them. John Ward lamented that the major-league owners would never "get over the idea that they owned us."

The NL and AA's victory over Ward and the Brotherhood was a Pyrrhic one. Both leagues were financially drained. The AA, however, was in worse shape, partly because of poor management and partly because it had never recovered from the ill-conceived expansion it had undertaken during the war against the UA. Sensing the weakness of their former rival, NL clubs began to violate the agreement that PL players would revert to their pre-1890 clubs. Boston signed star outfielder Harry Stovey, and Pittsburgh signed second baseman Louis Bierbauer; by rights, both players belonged to the AA Philadelphia Athletics. Because of its theft of Bierbauer, the Pittsburgh club is known to this day as the Pirates. After this, in a brief reprise of Monopoly War I, the AA and NL broke off relations and vigorously raided each other's rosters throughout the 1891 season.

Too weak to survive another war, the AA went belly up after the 1891 season. Strengthened by money it had received from the PL investors, the NL bought out the AA franchises in Baltimore, St. Louis, Washington, and Louisville for $130,000 and formed a new twelve-team league for the 1892 season. Once again William Hulbert's NL had the major-league monopoly all to itself. This time, Albert Spalding declared, the future would bring "permanent peace and prosperity."

As for John Montgomery Ward, he served as player-manager of Brooklyn's NL club for two years before returning to the Giants in the same capacity. Ward retired in 1894 to practice law full-time. He divorced his wife, Helen, in 1903, after they had been separated for years. Ward became wealthy from his Wall Street practice but never forgot his fellow baseball players. Throughout the 1890s and into the early twentieth century, Ward continued to represent major-league ballplayers who had been victimized by unscrupulous owners. In the late 1910s, Ward assisted in the Federal League's groundbreaking antitrust suit against major-league baseball. Amazingly enough, in 1909, the NL owners, who were certainly well acquainted with Ward's abilities, came within one vote of electing him league president.

A top-ranking amateur golfer in his later years, Ward died of pneumonia in 1925 in Augusta, Georgia, where he had gone to play in the celebrated Masters Tournament.

CHAPTER NINE

Casey at the Bat: Baseball in the Irish Decade

The game of professional baseball has always had a dark side. In the 1890s, however, baseball's dark side seemed to be a shade or two darker. Whether it was leftover bad feeling from the Players League revolt in 1890 and the death of the American Association in 1891, or a decade-long slump in the national economy, or what Al Spalding called "just personal cussedness and disregard for the future welfare of the game," baseball in the 1890s was often dreary, nasty, and mean-spirited.

This was particularly true off the field. Al Spalding and his fellow NL owners had realized their fondest dream by destroying both the PL and the AA. Beginning in 1892 the NL was once again the only game in town; the baseball monopoly was theirs and theirs alone. History had shown, however, that the monopoly was not necessarily good for the game of baseball—or even good for business. In times when two major leagues were competing with each other, as in the middle 1880s, baseball had thrived; in times when there was only one major league, as in the late 1870s, baseball had stagnated.

The first hint of a problem with the new twelve-team NL came when the final attendance figures were tabulated for the 1892 season. In 1891, a depressing year in which the NL had bled the AA to death by bidding up the salaries of its players, the average AA club had drawn 162,000 fans; this was only a little below the NL average of 166,000. Both figures were somewhat down from those of the late 1880s, but everyone expected the fans to forget the unpleasantness of the previous two seasons and come back in 1892.

It did not happen. In 1892 average attendance dropped even further, to 152,000. The NL was so worried that it started allowing clubs to schedule games on Sundays. For the rest of the decade the news was mixed. Overall league attendance rose from 1892 until 1896, but then began to fall; while there was an increase in attendance of 700,000 or so from 1892 to the end of the decade, the overall trend was not encouraging. NL clubs drew about half a million fewer fans in 1899 than they had in 1896.

What had gone wrong? Part of the problem was the inherent tedium of a twelve-team pennant race. A major-league executive once summed up what was wrong with baseball's ten-team, one-division structure in the early 1960s by asking: "How the hell do you sell a tenth-place team?" Every year of the 1890s, a pair of poor NL owners had to find a way to market teams that were in eleventh or twelfth place. Throughout the decade NL executives groped, with little success, for ways to recapture the excitement of the NL-AA rivalry of the 1880s.

In 1892 they tried a split-season format followed by a postseason playoff between the winner of the first half and the winner of the second half. That experiment failed. In the four years from 1894 to 1897 the NL played a postseason series called the Temple Cup, named after William C. Temple, the Pittsburgh sportsman who had donated the trophy. The Temple Cup series were best-four-of-seven-game playoffs between the first-place and second-place finishers in the regular season. The unavoidable problem with this arrangement was that the pennant winner had everything to lose and nothing to gain. In 1894 the Baltimore Orioles won the NL pennant by three games but lost the Temple Cup series to runner-up Boston, four games to none. Orioles third baseman John McGraw admitted that his team "didn't take the games too seriously. The regular season was over, and many of the boys made no effort to stay in condition." The Orioles were surprised and irritated, however, to discover that Boston was now claiming to be the real champions of baseball for 1894. Subsequent Temple Cup series never made anyone forget the thrilling St. Louis–Chicago World Series of 1886, and the cup was retired after 1897 for lack of fan interest.

It did not help that the 1890s were dominated by two great dynasties: the Baltimore Orioles and the Boston Beaneaters. These two teams won seven of the eight NL pennants between 1892 and 1899. At the other end of the standings, the NL in the 1890s featured some of the worst losing teams in the history of baseball. St. Louis went 39-111 in 1898; Louisville went 38-93 in 1896. The absolute worst NL team of all time, however, was the 1899 Cleveland Spiders.

The noncompetitiveness of many NL teams of the 1890s was not always an accident. In many cases it was the result of greedy owners who exploited the NL rule that allowed owners to have a financial interest in more than one franchise at a time. This led to the phenomenon of syndicate baseball, or common ownership of two or more teams. A good example of what was wrong

*The Boston Beaneaters of 1892, the first major-league
team to win 100 games*

with syndicate baseball is the story of the Cleveland
Spiders. Owned by trolley-car magnates Frank and
Stanley Robison, the Spiders had once been pennant-
contenders. Managed by Patsy Tebeau and led by such
stars as Cy Young, Cupid Childs, and outfielder Jesse
Burkett, who hit .410 to win the NL batting title, the
team finished in second place behind Baltimore in
1896. The Robisons, however, had their eye on greener
pastures in St. Louis, a larger market and a city that,
unlike Cleveland, permitted Sunday baseball. In 1899
the Robisons bought the St. Louis franchise from Chris
Von der Ahe and began to transfer talent from Cleve-

141

land to St. Louis. St. Louis improved and rose from last place to fifth. Cleveland, however, compiled a record of 20-134.

One of the most abysmal performances in major-league history, the Cleveland Spiders' 1899 season was actually even worse than it looked; because twelve of the team's twenty victories came in doubleheader splits, there were only eight days during the season when the Spiders did not lose. The team had six losing streaks of eleven games or more and had only one winning streak—of two games. Cleveland finished the season 84 games behind first-place Brooklyn, embarrassing the NL so badly that the team was dropped from the league after the season, along with fellow losers Louisville, Washington, and Baltimore. The loss of these cities would come back to haunt the NL during the next monopoly war, however. Both Louisville and Baltimore were victims of syndicate baseball. In many cases, clubs did not even try to cover up the clear conflicts of interest caused by syndicate baseball; at one point in the late 1890s Ned Hanlon was simultaneously the manager of one NL team, the Brooklyn Superbas, and president of another, the Baltimore Orioles. Washington was run by an owner so inconsiderate of his fans that in 1899 he moved all of the team's home games with the Phillies to Philadelphia, because Philadelphia drew better.

With syndicate baseball and owners like the Robisons, the 1890s was not an easy decade for baseball fans—or for major-league players. With the PL, the AA, and the Brotherhood out of the way, the NL came down hard on the players. In 1892 rosters were reduced and salaries were slashed by 30 or even 40 percent. A number of players, including top-ranking pitchers Charlie Buffinton and Silver King, quit baseball when they found that they could make a better living outside of the game. Major-league owners treated even the biggest stars in baseball with disdain.

Andrew Freedman was one of the worst owners. A shady associate of New York City's Tammany Hall political machine, Freedman bought the New York Giants in 1895. One of his first acts was to fine the team's biggest star, pitcher Amos Rusie, $200—almost 10 percent of his salary—for his supposedly poor effort late in the season. An indignant Rusie refused to pitch unless the money was returned and ended up sitting out the entire 1896 season. John Ward took up Rusie's cause and appealed to the league, but was rejected. With the 1897 season approaching, however, and Rusie threatening to bring an antitrust suit against major-league baseball—the Sherman Antitrust Act, the first federal antitrust law, had been passed by Congress in 1890—Freedman's fellow owners became nervous. Unable to budge the stubborn Freedman, they passed the hat and paid Rusie his entire 1896 salary themselves. Rusie returned to New York and in 1897 went 29-8 with a league-leading ERA of 2.54.

Even the venerable Cap Anson was not too sacred a figure to be abused by the men who ran major-league baseball in the 1890s. Expecting to take over as president of the Chicago White Stockings when Al Spalding retired, Anson was shocked in 1891 when Spalding named James Hart as his successor instead. Hart wanted Anson out as manager and when, in 1897, Anson refused to resign, Hart fired him. Anson batted .302 in his twenty-second—and final—NL season; he had played all twenty-two of those seasons with the Chicago White Stockings. After being fired, Anson claimed that Spalding had promised him a chance to buy the team and had gone back on his word. When Spalding responded by offering to sponsor a public benefit to raise money for Anson's retirement, an angry Anson refused, saying that he would not accept anything "in the nature of a charity." Anson explained later that, "as I was not a pauper, the public owed me nothing." Left unsaid was what he felt Spalding owed him. In his 1900 autobiography, *A Ball Player's Career*, a disillusioned Cap Anson wrote:

> *From personal experience I know that the National Game was never in as healthy condition as it was when the League had the old American Association for a rival and when such a thing as syndicate base-ball was unheard of. The Harts, the Friedmans [sic] and the Robisons were not then in control, and the rule-or-ruin policy that now prevails had at that time not even been thought of.*
>
> *Base-ball as at present conducted is a gigantic monopoly, intolerant of opposition and run on a grab-all-that-there-is-in-sight policy that is alienating its friends and disgusting the very public that has so long and cheerfully given to it the support that it has withheld from other forms of amusement.*[1]

Another self-inflicted problem with major-league baseball in the 1890s was that it had shrunk geographically. Starting in 1892, the game was played in only a fraction of the cities that had hosted major-league clubs during the two-league and three-league seasons of the 1880s. Between 1882 and 1890, there were major-league franchises, at one time or another, in twenty-six different cities: Boston, Baltimore, Buffalo, Chicago, Cincinnati, Cleveland, Detroit, Indianapolis, Kansas City, New York, Philadelphia, Pittsburgh, Providence, St. Louis, Troy, Washington, Worcester, Brooklyn, Columbus, Louisville, Richmond, Toledo, Altoona, Milwaukee, Saint Paul, and Wilmington. Several of these cities had more than one club; some had two clubs in different leagues at the same time. When the NL adopted the twelve-team one-league format in

1892, it shut large areas of the country—and millions of fans—out of the world of major-league baseball.

The changes of 1891 and 1892 also reflect a shift in major-league power and influence back to the East. The NL had begun as a rebellion of primarily western interests against an eastern clique; now the pendulum was swinging back. A disproportionate number of the disenfranchised major-league cities and regions were in the West. Six of the clubs in the new NL were located on the East Coast: Baltimore, New York, Brooklyn, Boston, Philadelphia, and Washington; and three—Cincinnati, Pittsburgh, and Louisville—were in the gray area between East and West. Only Chicago, St. Louis, and arguably Cleveland could have been called western cities in 1892. This would also be a factor in the next monopoly war.

This geographical shrinking led to cultural changes as well. It is no coincidence that major-league baseball in the 1890s was dominated by the Irish, who had immigrated to America in greater and greater numbers from the late 1840s until the late 1880s, most of them settling in large eastern cities. Baseball had always had its share of Irish-born players, many of them ex-cricketers, like Andy Leonard from County Cavan, Tommy Bond from Granard, and Tom Foley from Cashel, all of whom played in the National Association in the 1870s. In the late 1880s and the 1890s, however, a new wave of mostly second-generation Irishmen virtually took over baseball. Irish-surnamed players had made up about 25 percent of all major-league players in the mid-1880s; ten years later that figure had increased to between 40 and 50 percent.

On the better teams the percentage of Irishmen seemed to be even higher. The Baltimore Orioles had Hanlon, McGraw, Keeler, Jennings, Kelley, McMahon, Brouthers, Brodie, Robinson, Doyle, and McGann; the Boston Beaneaters had Selee, McCarthy, Duffy, Nash,

Kelly, Collins, and Hamilton. Unable to explain this Irish invasion of baseball, some sportswriters of the 1890s suggested that the Irish were somehow biologically superior to other nationalities, especially in the area of foot speed. Others attributed the success of the Irish to cheating and physical intimidation of their opponents.

While these views reflect an anti-Irish bigotry that was typical of the United States in the nineteenth century, the dog-eat-dog spirit that characterized the business side of major-league baseball in the 1890s does seem to have filtered down to the game on the field. Baseball in the Irish decade was filled with violence, bad sportsmanship, and ear-blistering profanity. Speaking, with characteristic understatement, of the differences between the game played by the Beaneaters and Orioles and the baseball of his day, George Wright observed, "It is impossible for a respectable woman to go to a ball game in the National League without running the risk of hearing language which is disgraceful."

That was certainly true if the woman was sitting within earshot of the umpire. Manager Ned Hanlon of the Orioles, in particular, transformed the "kicking" of Anson and Comiskey into something much more menacing. As one contemporary Cleveland sportswriter put it, "the national game never received so severe a setback as it did during the last Baltimore series here . . . In ten years' experience in scoring games in Cleveland, I have never seen such a torrent of vulgarity, profanity and brutal senseless abuse heaped upon an umpire as Lynch stood from the Baltimore players." Former umpire John Heydler, who served as president of the NL in the 1920s, later described the Baltimore style from personal experience: "The Orioles were mean, vicious, ready at any time to maim a rival player or an umpire, if it helped their cause. The things they would say to an umpire were unbelievably vile, and they broke the

146

spirit of some fine men. I've seen umpires bathe their feet by the hour after McGraw and others spiked them through their shoes."[2]

There was, of course, a positive side to the 1890s. If the great Irish-dominated teams of the decade sometimes crossed the line into bullying and rowdyism, they also played a fast-paced, tactically creative, run-and-gun style of baseball that continues to influence the way major-league baseball is played today. Like the game of the 1980s and 1990s, baseball 1890s-style featured great base stealers like Sliding Billy Hamilton, who hit .344 lifetime, stole 937 bases, and scored 1,692 runs in 1,593 games; great hitters for average like Wee Willie Keeler, a singles hitter who from 1894 to 1899 batted .391, .392, .432, .379, and .377; and great power hitters like Big Ed Delahanty, who hit .345 lifetime, led the NL in doubles five times, and reached double figures in triples ten times. Even though the double and triple were the power statistics of the 1890s— few ballparks had home run fences that could be reached by a long fly ball—Delahanty was still strong enough to hit nineteen home runs in one season and thirteen in another.

Managed by Frank Selee, Boston had defensive third basemen Billy Nash and his successor Jimmy Collins; both were virtuosos at fielding the bunt, which was used in the 1890s primarily as a means of getting on base, not as a sacrifice. Selee's club was one of the first to use what was called "offensive teamwork." Using a complicated set of signals that could originate from the runner, the batter, or the bench, the Beaneaters worked the hit and run play in a bewildering series of variations. Boston's outfield featured the "Heavenly Twins," Tommy McCarthy and Hugh Duffy; both hit for average and could run. In 1894 Duffy had one of the great offensive stat lines in history, collecting 236 hits, 50 doubles, 18 home runs, 145 RBIs, 49 stolen bases, and a .438 batting average; he was the league leader in every one of these categories except stolen bases. The five-foot-seven-inch, 168-pound Duffy had surprising power; he led the league in home runs twice and drove in 100 or more runs seven years in a row. Selee's Boston Beaneaters won the NL pennant in 1892, 1893, 1897, and 1898; in 1892 they became the first team ever to win 100 games, finishing the season at 102-48.

Ned Hanlon's Baltimore Orioles interrupted Boston's run of pennants by taking the NL flag in 1894, 1895, and 1896. The Orioles had great players like sluggers Dan Brouthers and Joe Kelley, catcher Wilbert Robinson, and table-setters and run scorers John McGraw and Wee Willie Keeler, but they have gone down in history as the dirtiest team ever. They were supposed to have hidden extra balls in the high outfield grass for outfielders to use when the real ball got by them, and they supposedly grabbed base runners' belts and spiked their feet as they were rounding bases.

While at least some of these stories appear to be true, the Orioles invented many legal tactics as well. They had their own versions of the hit and run, including a play with leadoff man John McGraw on first, in which McGraw would break for second with the pitch, and number two batter Wee Willie Keeler would lay a bunt down the third base line. Whether Keeler beat the play at first base or not, McGraw would continue past second base and reach third easily before the third baseman could get back. McGraw and Keeler also perfected the art of hitting the ball straight down into a patch of dirt which the Orioles would intentionally keep dry and hard; the ball would bounce so high that opposing infielders would have no play on the batter going down to first. Known as the Baltimore chop, this technique has made a comeback in the age of AstroTurf.

As baseball historian Lee Allen wrote, "the Orioles were great players . . . but their greatness stemmed from sheer ability. They were titans in spite of and not because of their titanic boorishness."[3] In spite of the ugliness and meanness of the game in the 1890s, something of the competitive spirit of baseball's Irish decade did survive and outlive that "era of tobacco-chewing profanity" in the person of the many players of the 1890s who went on to become managers in the twentieth century. Jimmy Collins, Hugh Duffy, Hughie Jennings, Kid Gleason, Tommy McCarthy, Wilbert Robinson, and Joe Kelley are just a few of the Beaneaters and Orioles who later managed major-league clubs. The two greatest baseball minds of the twentieth century were also products of the Irish decade. They are ex-Oriole John McGraw, who won ten National League pennants and three world championships with the New York Giants between 1902 and 1932, and Connie Mack—born Cornelius McGillicuddy—who managed the Philadelphia Athletics in the American League for an incredible fifty-three years, winning nine pennants and five world championships.

SOURCE NOTES

CHAPTER TWO
1. Lee Allen, *The National League Story* (New York: Hill and Wang, 1961), p. 4.
2. Albert Spalding, *America's National Game*, rev. and ed. by Samm Combs and Bob West (San Francisco: Halo Books, 1991), pp. 124–25.

CHAPTER THREE
1. MacLean Kennedy, *The Great Teams of Baseball* (St. Louis: Sporting News, 1928), p. 13.
2. Gerald Astor, ed., *The Baseball Hall of Fame 50th Anniversary Book* (New York: Prentice Hall, 1988), p. 22.
3. Albert Spalding, *America's National Game*, rev. and ed. by Samm Combs and Bob West (San Francisco: Halo Books, 1991), p. 167.

CHAPTER FOUR
1. Harold Seymour, *Baseball: The Early Years* (New York: Oxford University Press, 1960), p. 106.
2. Seymour, p. 140.

CHAPTER FIVE
1. Craig Wright and Tom Nouse, *The Diamond Appraised* (New York: Simon and Schuster, 1989), p. 154.
2. Peter Levine, *A. G. Spalding and the Rise of Baseball* (New York: Oxford University Press, 1985), p. 43.
3. G. W. Axelson, *Commy* (Chicago: Reilly and Lee, 1919), p. 90.

CHAPTER SIX
1. John Thorn and John Holway, *The Pitcher* (New York: Prentice Hall, 1987), pp. 150–51.
2. Irving Leitner, *Baseball, Diamond in the Rough* (New York: Criterion Books, 1972), p. 173.

CHAPTER SEVEN
1. Jerry Malloy "The National Pastime," SABR; Fall 1982, p. 18.

CHAPTER EIGHT
1. Albert Spalding, *America's National Game*, rev. and ed. by Samm Combs and Bob West (San Francisco: Halo Books, 1991), p. 171.
2. Spalding, pp. 171–72.

CHAPTER NINE
1. Adrian Anson, *A Ball Player's Career* (Mattituck, N.Y.: Amereon House, n.d.), p. 329.
2. Charles Alexander, *John McGraw* (New York: Viking, 1988), p. 55.
3. Lee Allen, *100 Years of Baseball* (New York: Bartholomew House, 1950), p. 131.

BIBLIOGRAPHY

Alexander, Charles. *John McGraw*. New York: Viking, 1988.

Allen, Lee. *100 Years of Baseball*. New York: Bartholomew House, 1950.

_____ *Hot Stove League*. New York: A. S. Barnes, 1955.

_____ *The National League Story*. New York: Hill and Wang, 1961.

Anson, Adrian. *A Ballplayer's Career 1960*. Mattituck, N.Y.: Amereon House (repr.), n.d.

Axelson, G. W. *Commy*. Chicago: Reilly and Lee, 1919.

Gershman, Michael. *Diamonds: The Evolution of the Ballpark*. Boston: Houghton Mifflin, 1993.

James, Bill. *The Bill James Historical Baseball Abstract*. New York: Villard Books, 1988.

Kennedy, MacLean. *The Great Teams of Baseball*. St. Louis: The Sporting News, 1928.

Leitner, Irving. *Baseball, Diamond in the Rough*. New York: Criterion Books, 1972.

Levine, Peter. *A. G. Spalding and the Rise of Baseball*. New York: Oxford University Press, 1985.

Lowenfish, Lee, and Tony Lupien. *The Imperfect Diamond*. New York: Stein and Day, 1980.

Obojski, Robert. *Bush League*. New York: Macmillan, 1975.

Orem, Preston D. *Baseball (1845–1881) from the Newspaper Accounts*. Altadena: Self-published, 1961.

Quigley, Martin. *The Crooked Pitch*. Chapel Hill: Algonquin Books, 1984.

Ryczek, William. *Blackguards and Red Stockings, A History of Baseball's National Association, 1871-1875*. Jefferson, N.C.: McFarland, 1992.

Seymour, Harold. *Baseball: The Early Years*. New York: Oxford University Press, 1960.

Spalding, Albert. *Base Ball, America's National Game*, rev. and ed. Samm Combs and Bob West. San Francisco: Halo Books, 1991.

Thorn, John, and John Holway. *The Pitcher*. New York: Prentice-Hall, 1987.

Thorn, John, and Pete Palmer, eds. *Total Baseball*, 3d ed. New York: Harper Collins, 1993.

Tygiel, Jules. *Baseball's Great Experiment*. New York: Oxford University Press, 1983.

Zoss, Joel, and John Bowman. *Diamonds in the Rough*. New York: Macmillan, 1989.

INDEX

Duffy, Hugh, 111, 133, 147, 149

Eight-team league, 30
ERA, 16, 24, 29, 53, 64, 70, 77, 78, 80, 81, 85, 92, 96, 98, 102, 103, 107, 109–111, 125, 143, 149

Fair-foul hit, 16, 17, 30, 37
Farm system, 49
Ferguson, Robert, 19, 26
Flint, Frank "Silver," 36, 37, 40, 42, 43
Force, Davy, 12, 13–15, 24
Fowler, John "Bud," 116–120, 121, 123
Franchises, 12, 26, 28–33, 57, 61–62, 65–69, 71, 118, 128, 132, 134–136, 140, 141, 144

Galvin, Pud, 104, 107, 120, 133
Gambling, 8–11, 26, 28–30, 44, 62
Game attendance, 12, 30, 70, 71, 88, 128, 133, 134, 139
Glasscock, Jack, 69, 134
Gloveless fielders.
See Bare-handed fielders
Gloves, 16, 40, 44, 73, 105
Goldsmith, Fred, 36, 37, 52, 100, 102

Gore, George, 35, 37, 44, 45, 82, 131
Grant, Frank, 117, 120, 121
Grays, 76, 78–81
Great Fire, 20, 21

Hall of Fame.
See National Baseball Hall of Fame and Museum
Hartford Dark Blues, 100
Hecker, Guy, 64, 77, 103, 119
Henderson, Rickey, 43, 97
Hidden-ball trick, 19
Hines, Paul, 37, 77
Home runs, 38, 39, 41, 42, 64, 77, 85, 96, 126, 147
Hulbert, William A., 15, 20–21, 27–28, 32, 36–37, 41, 47, 56, 62, 63, 66

International League (IL), 116, 117, 119–121, 122, 144
Investors, 57, 131, 132, 135, 136
Irish players, 31, 42, 54, 103, 104, 138, 145, 146, 148, 149

Keefe, Tim, 77, 78, 81, 92, 103, 107, 115, 126
Keeler, Wee Willie, 147, 148

158